INTERNATIONAL RELATIONS

Volume 3, United Nations

Jack E. Vincent

Professor of Political Science
Florida Atlantic University
Boca Raton, Florida 33432

UNIVERSITY
PRESS OF
AMERICA

LANHAM • NEW YORK • LONDON

Library of Congress Cataloging in Publication Data

Vincent, Jack Ernest.
    International relations.

    Contents: v. 1. Law–v. 2. Structures–v. 3. United
Nations.–v. 4. Theory
    1. International relations. 2. International law. I. Title.
JX1391.V56   1983   327   83–3541
ISBN 0–8191–3160–1 (pbk. : v. 1)
ISBN 0–8191–3193–8 (pbk. : v. 2)
ISBN 0–8191–3163–6 (pbk. : v. 3)
ISBN 0–8191–3194–6 (pbk. : v. 4)

Author's Note: The purpose of this volume is to present, in non-technical and concise terms, the essentials of the United Nations system. Companion volumes for law, other structures, such as OAS, and theory are available from the same publisher. A bibliography for all volumes is found in the theory volume.

VOLUME 3, THE UNITED NATIONS SYSTEM

Index

Introduction, p.3
Historic Background, p.4
The Charter of the United Nations, p.8
Decision Making in the United Nations, p.10
Groupings in the United Nations, p.11
United Nations Delegates and their Protections, p.12
Nation Membership in the United Nations, p.13
Assessments of Members, p.15
Major Organs of the United Nations, p.17
General Assembly, p.18
Security Council, p.37
Economic and Social Council, p.48
Specialized and Other Agencies, p.57
Responsibilities for Non-Self Governing Territories, p.82
International Court of Justice, p.88
Secretariat, p.116
The Charter, p.119

Introduction

The United Nations came into formal existence on October 24, 1945. Its Charter was drafted by delegates of fifty nations which met in San Francisco from April 25 - June 26, 1945. The General Assembly held its first session on January 10, 1946.

The United Nations is the second major collective security experiment in this century, the first being the League of Nations. Basically, the United Nations may be viewed as a resurrection of the League, but with certain modifications to fill the gaps and deficiencies of the League system.

First, states pledge, upon becoming members of the United Nations, that they will not use force or the threat of force against the territorial integrity and political independence of other states, except in their own self-defense. In short, the United Nations system seems to illegalize "a state of war," defined as a situation of equal co-belligerency. This stands in contrast to the legal situation in the League system where war was allowable under certain circumstances until 1928.

Second, under the United Nations system, states give the Security Council the right to make a determination as to whether the Charter has been violated and they pledge to support the decisions of the Security Council. In the League system, on the other hand, each state decided for itself whether the Covenant had been violated and whether sanctions should be applied, although the League Council could make recommendations in these respects.

Third, it was envisioned at San Francisco that the United Nations would acquire a military force donated by member states, under the control of the Security Council, to be used in the maintenance of peace and security. In the League system, on the other hand, any collective enforcement action stayed in national hands.

Fourth, many of the procedures of the United Nations are more liberal, from a supranational point of view, than those of the League of Nations. In particular, the United Nations employs (basically) a majority voting system for both the Security Council and General Assembly. This stands in contrast to the unanimity system of the League Council and Assembly. Although the five permanent members of the Security Council do possess a veto over most Council decisions, in the League system, every state, that was not a party to a dispute, possessed such a privilege in Council and the Assembly.

Finally, the basic principles of the League collective security system are modified. In the League system it was assumed that all states would react against any aggressor while in the United Nations system special emphasis is put upon the responsibilities of the permanent members of the Security Council. Thus, the fundamental principle of the League may be characterized

as "all peace-loving against the few aggressors" while the UN
principle might be characterized as "the big against the middle
sized and small."

Although the United Nations can be seen, thus far, as more
successful in accomplishing its objectives than the League,
nevertheless, it is clear that the framers at San Francisco
misjudged the readiness of states to accept the new system.

First, they misjudged the willingness of states to place
permanent military contingents under the United Nations. As the
system has worked out, the United Nations does not possess a much
stronger collective security capability, defined as standing
forces, than the League did.

Second, they misjudged the readiness of the permanent members
of the Security Council to cooperate with one another in respect
to peace and security matters. The permanent members of the
Security Council are frequently at loggerheads over, and
frequently deeply involved in, the very crises that they were,
presumably, to resolve.

Third, they misjudged the willingness of states generally to
support the collective security principle. Thus, the United
Nations has seen little more support of collective security
actions than was the case in the League. The most important "test
case" in this regard was the Korean conflict which saw a number of
states ignoring the UN or actually aiding the side opposite to
which the United Nations was committed.

In general, there has been a tendency for many states to
return to the classical state behavior patterns evidenced in the
League system and before it. There is a tendency for states to
create alliances, which make inroads into collective security
pledges--in the sense that it is unlikely that military allies
will act against one another. Also, there seems to be a tendency
to engage in action outside of the United Nations framework in
order to accomplish objectives. Historic examples include: the
US-British military actions during the Lebanon crisis (1958), the
US military action in the Dominican Republic (1965) and Vietnam
(1965-1973), the French-British-Israeli invasion of Egypt (1956),
the USSR's action in Hungary (1956), Czechoslovakia (1968), and
Afghanistan (1979), and the Indian "conquest" of the Portugese enclaves of Goa, Diu and Damao (1961).

On the other hand, it cannot be said that the United Nations
has been without effect upon the behavior of states since World
War II. It seems fairly clear that it has had distinctly
pacifying effect on a number of important crises; most notably,
Korea, Suez, Congo, and Cyprus. Further, the United Nations has
served as an important channel of communication between states and
a funnel through which funds and technical assistance are given to
the bulk of the underdeveloped countries of the world.

Historic Background

Although the League of Nations system had failed to prevent World War II, there was strong sentiment during the war in favor of generating a "new" system, based on the same basic principles. Important in this regard was the Connally Resolution of November 5, 1943, initiated by Senator Tom Connally of Texas. The resolution expressed the commitment of the Senate of the United States to recognizing "the necessity of there being established at the earliest practical date a general international organization, based on the principle of the sovereign equality of all peace-loving states, and open to the membership of all such states, large and small, for the maintenance of international peace and security." The Connally Resolution passed eighty-five to five. Although it was not binding upon individual senators in respect to their vote to commit the United States to the United Nations Charter, nevertheless, its passage clearly revealed the Senate support for the United Nations. This stands in contrast to the earlier rejection of the League of Nations by the Senate.

Important prior steps leading to the adoption of the Charter at San Francisco were: (1) the construction and failure of the League of Nations system; (2) the issuance in August, 1941, of the "Atlantic Charter"; (3) the endorsement of the Atlantic Charter by twenty-six allied powers, in January, 1942, in their "Declaration by United Nations"; (4) a commitment by the United States, United Kingdom, USSR and China to construct a "general international organization . . . for the maintenance of international peace and security" in their "Moscow Declaration" of October, 1943; (5) an agreement on the broad outlines of the United Nations by the United States, United Kingdom, USSR, and China at the Dumbarton Oaks Conference of August-October, 1944; and (6) an agreement on certain unsolved details, particularly the question of the "veto" power, by the United States, USSR, and the United Kingdom, at the Yalta Conference of February, 1945.

These steps show that the document was primarily the work of "great powers," and this fact is reflected in the powers and responsibilities of the members and the UN organs, particularly in respect to the predominance of the Security Council in peace and security matters and the permanent presence of the great powers on that organ. The influence of the smaller and medium powers was also felt at San Francisco, especially on the matters of keeping the composition of the Security Council's agenda and the discussion of it "veto free" and the question of enlarging the scope, role, and status of the Economic and Social Council and the Trusteeship Council.

The purposes of the organization, as agreed upon at San Francisco, are as follows:

1. maintain international peace and security, and, to that end: to take effective collective measures for the prevention and removal of threats to the peace, and for the suppression of acts of aggression or other

breaches of the peace, and to bring about
by peaceful means, and in conformity
with the principles of justice and international law, adjustment or settlement of
international disputes or situations which
might lead to a breach of the peace;

2. to develop friendly relations among nations based on respect for the principle
of equal rights and self-determination of
peoples, and to take other appropriate
measures to strengthen universal peace;

3. to achieve international cooperation in
solving international problems of an
economic, social, cultural, or humanitarian
character, and in promoting and encouraging respect for human rights and for fundamental freedoms for all without distinction as to race, sex, language, or religion;
and;

4. to be a center for harmonizing the actions
of nations in the attainment of these common
ends. (Charter, Article 1)

After the UN Charter was approved at the April-June, 1945 San
Francisco Conference attended by fifty states, a Preparatory
Commission was created to make arrangements for the first meetings
of the United Nations' principal organs. It was composed of all
of the original signers of the Charter, but much of the work was
accomplished by an Executive Committee consisting of the USSR,
United States, Great Britain, China, France, Canada,
Czechoslovakia, Chile, Brazil, Australia, Iran, Yugoslavia,
Netherlands, and Mexico. The Executive Committee submitted a
report to the full Commission in November, 1945. The report, with
some revision, became recommendations to the major United Nations
organs during their first meetings in 1946. Many of the present
rules of procedure are based on the recommendations of the
Preparatory Commission.

In this connection, there were certain important
transitional and other agreements provided for in the Charter.
For example, Article 106 of the Charter empowers the permanent
members of the Security Council to "consult with one another and
as the occasion requires with other Members of the United Nations
with a view to such joint action on behalf of the Organization as
may be necessary for the purpose of maintaining international
peace and security." This privilege is qualified by the proviso
that it may be exercised "pending the coming into force of such
special agreements referred to in Article 43" (Article 43 concerns
the placing of national military contingents under the Security
Council). Because the provisions of Article 43 have never come
into effect, from a purely technical point of view the permanent
members of the Council can presumably still rely on Article 106.

However, because Article 106 has never been used, it would be best
to consider it obsolete. In any case, this article cannot be
considered to allow the unilateral action by one of the permanent
members because it only authorizes "joint action on behalf of the
organization>."
        Another transitional matter was treated in Article 107 which
provides "nothing in the present Charter shall invalidate or
preclude action, in relation to any state which during the Second
World War has been an enemy of any signatory to the present
Charter, taken or authorized as a result of that war by the
Governments having responsibility for such action." Presumably,
although not clearly, these provisions cease to apply when an
enemy state regains its status as an ordinary member of the
International community through a peace treaty. At present, then,
this article seems to apply only to Germany. In that no final
peace treaty has been signed concerning Germany, can several
states, including the USSR and the United Sates, take action
against Germany without violating the Charter? From one
perspective, it would seem that such action is legally possible.
However, it would seem that time has eroded the readiness of
states to accept the implications of this Article. On the other
hand, during the Berlin Crisis of 1948 the Soviet Union maintained
that action could be taken by the USSR in regard to her occupation
zone in Germany without it becoming a concern of the United
Nations. Also, the Warsaw Pact, directed against Western Germany,
is based in part upon Article 107. Article 107 is tied to Article
53 which provides:
        no enforcement action shall be taken under regional
        arrangements or by regional agencies without the
        authorization of the Security Council, with the exception of
        measures against any enemy state. . .provided for pursuant to
        Article 107 or in regional arrangements directed against
        renewal of aggressive policy on the part of any such state,
        until such time as the Organization may, on request of the
        Governments concerned, be charged with the responsibility for
        preventing further aggression by such a state.
Since the USSR has never requested that the Organization take
responsibility in respect to Germany, from the USSR's perspective,
possible Warsaw Pact action against West Germany is excepted from
the above requirement of Security Council authorization.
        Also important was the effort to prevent the formation of
"secret treaties," which many statesmen felt were important causes
of international conflict. Article 102 of the Charter provides
that all treaties and international agreements entered into after
the signing of the Charter must be "as soon as possible registered
with the Secretariat and published by it." This provision, found
also in the Covenant, reflects the Wilsonian idea that all
treaties and agreements should be "open" to prevent the kind of
secret diplomatic bargains that occurred before and during World
War I. In the Charter, a sanction is provided to encourage

compliance with this provision, in that any agreements or treaties which are not registered cannot be invoked "before any organ of the United Nations." Thus, an unregistered treaty can not be cited in a case before the International Court of Justice nor in connection with decisions of the Security Council. This does not prevent other non-United Nations tribunals, however, from considering such treaties as a component of international law. In this respect, the Charter provisions differ markedly from those of the Covenant because, in the case of the latter, unregistered treaties were not "binding until so registered" (Covenant, Article 18). At present, in spite of these provisions, states frequently engage in agreements that are not registered with the Secretariat and, therefore, not published. Many of these unregistered agreements concern the alliances of East and West. Exact state responsibilities in the event of a conflict as to who will do what, when, and where, are, of course, presently tantamount to military secrets, and, in spite of the fact that they are international agreements, are not registered with the Secretariat. It is apparent that the sanction provided for is not a sufficient inducement to overcome the apparent sense of security derived from keeping these agreements unregistered, in violation of the Charter. On the other hand, states do adhere to the letter of the Charter in respect to the more general alliance commitments they have undertaken (i.e., the texts of the NATO Treaty and the Warsaw Pact Treaty are duly registered).

The Charter of the United Nations

Article 103 establishes the pre-eminence of the UN Charter over any other international obligation. It stipulates "in the event of a conflict between the obligations of the Members of the United Nations and of the present Charter and their obligations under any other international agreement, their obligations under the Charter shall prevail." For example, if a state were to enter into agreement so that it was obligated not to view the Security Council's decisions under Article 41 as binding, such an obligation itself would not be binding in the legal sense because of Article 103. Thus, although the Charter is a treaty, it is a treaty of a special kind which, short of amendment to change this provision, has priority over future treaties in a way not unlike a constitution's priority over ordinary law. In the case of ordinary treaties, they can simply be overturned by future treaties as municipal ordinary laws can be overturned by new laws.

The Charter also provides for the objectives, procedures, and organs, within the United Nations system.

In signing the Charter, members pledge, among other things, to: (1) respect the "sovereign equality" of other members; (2) settle their international disputes by "peaceful means" so that "international peace and security, and justice, are not endangered"; (3) refrain from the "threat or the use of force against the territorial integrity or political independence of any state, or in any other manner inconsistent with the Purposes of the United Nations"; and (4) give the United Nations "assistance" in action it undertakes in accordance with the Charter and "refrain from giving assistance to any state against which the United Nations is taking preventive or enforcement action." (Article 2)

Other articles treat: Membership; major organs; pacific settlement of disputes; actions with respect to threats and breaches of the peace and acts of aggression; regional arrangements; international, economic, and social cooperation; non-self-governing territories; the trusteeship system; miscellaneous provisions; transitional security arrangements; and ratifications.

Amendments of the Charter come into force after having been voted for adoption by two-thirds of the members of the General Assembly and ratification by two-thirds of the member states including all of the permanent members of the Security Council. Thus, each permanent member of the Security Council possesses a veto over possible amendments. Amendments are binding on all member states, whether ratified by them or not. However, unfavorable amendments, as viewed at the San Francisco Conference, may be grounds for withdrawal from the organization. Since the tenth annual session, a conference to review the Charter can be called by a majority vote of the General Assembly and a procedural vote of the Security Council (no veto). Prior to the tenth session, such a conference required a two-thirds vote in the General Assembly and a procedural vote in the Security Council. When and if a conference is held, proposed amendments will come into force when ratified by two-thirds of the Members including all of the permanent members of the Security Council. Amendments proposed in 1963 by the General Assembly to increase the membership of the Security Council and Economic and Social Council, came into legal effect after sufficient ratifications, on August 31, 1965. An additional amendment, which doubled the membership of the Economic and Social Council, was ratified in 1973. Expansion of memberships has been spurred by the interest in allowing greater representation of the newer countries in Asia and Africa.

Chapters VI and VII are of particular importance to the peacekeeping mission of the United Nations. These provisions refer to international situations and disputes that are serious enough to be "likely to endanger international peace and security." They are not so dangerous, however, as to actually constitute a threat to the peace, a breach of the peace, or an act of aggression (treated in Chapter VII). Both the Security Council and the General Assembly are treated in Chapter VI, in the sense that situations and disputes may be brought to their attention. Only the Security Council is mentioned, however, in the detailed procedural provisions of Chapter VI. Presumably then, the General Assembly is free from the various procedural restrictions put upon the Security Council in Chapter VII in respect to the treatment of disputes and situations; although the General Assembly cannot make recommendations on disputes or situations being considered by the Security Council unless the Security Council so requests (Article 12 (1)). Because the matters treated in Chapter VI are less serious than those covered in Chapter VII, the Security Council and the General Assembly are limited to Chapter VI to making recommendations. When the Security Council applies chapter VI, however, members of the Security Council must "abstain" from voting (permanent members lose their veto) if they are a party to a dispute. On the other hand, any voting determination concerning whether to operate under Chapter VI is subject to the veto.

Chapter VII, in contrast, details Security Council responsibilities in respect to the collective security functions of the United Nations. Chapter VII only applies when the Security Council has determined that there is a "threat to the peace," a "breach of the peace," or "acts of aggression" in the international community. Such a determination stands in contrast to that made in connection with Chapter VI concerning disputes and situations "likely" to endanger international peace and security. The Security Council is empowered under Chapter VII to make recommendations; restore peace and security (Article 39); call upon disputants to comply with provisional measures (i.e., cease fire, Article 40) and/or make decisions in respect to non-military measures (i.e., severance of economic relations, Article 41) and/or military measures (Article 42). The failure of the Military Staff Committee to secure arrangements for armed forces contributions to be made to the Security Council, provided by Article 43, however, limits the Security Council, at present, to deciding upon non-military measures and recommending military measures. Although the General Assembly is not mentioned in Chapter VII, the Uniting for Peace Resolution seems to give the Assembly the same recommendation powers, instead of decision powers (qualified above), provided for in Articles 41 and 42.

Decision Making in the United Nations

As noted above, the General Assembly is limited to making recommendations, which can be contrasted with a decision. A recommendation is the equivalent of a suggestion and, therefore, technically, has no legal consequences. This is not to say that recommendations may not have considerable political significance. Nevertheless, a state does not violate international law when it refuses to honor a United Nations recommendation.

A decision, in contrast to a recommendation, is considered binding upon states and, therefore, is similar to a rule of international law. In the United Nations system, only the International Court of Justice and the Security Council are empowered to make decisions. Whenever the Court has jurisdiction and decides a case or provisional measures, a state is considered

to have committed a delict (a violation of law) if it refused
compliance. The Security Council makes decisions binding on
states only when it operates under Article 41, which applies to
non-forceful collective security measures, and Article 42,
pertaining to forceful collective security measures. The latter
provisions, however, are contingent upon the establishemnt of
special agreements between force contributing states and the
Security Council. Because these agreements have never come into
effect, the Security Council is limited to making decisions in
respect to Article 41 but only recommendations in respect to
Article 42. Although the term "decide" is used elsewhere in the
Charter it does not refer, in these cases, to "decisions"
binding upon states (i.e., the Security Council may "decide" to
operate under Article 36, allowing recommendations as to the mode
of pacific settlement, if parties to a dispute refer a dispute to
the Security Council).

One other category of procedure, "call upon" measures, may
either have the character of a recommendation or a decision,
depending upon the provisions of the Charter relied upon. Because
the General Assembly is limited to making recommendations, anytime
states are "called upon" to do something by the General Assembly,
they are free, technically, to refuse compliance. When the
Security Council is operating under provisions other than those in
Chapter VII its "call upon" measures seem to have the same weight
as those of the General Assembly. However, when states are
"called upon" in respect to provisional measures (Article 40),
non-military, collective enforcement (Article 41), and collective
military enforcement (Article 42, 43), the Security Council
"request" is binding and has the same status as rule of
international law.

Groupings in the United Nations

Caucusing groups are organizations of member states which meet
with some degree of regularity for the purpose of discussing
questions and issues connected with the United Nations. Most
important caucusing groups, that is: the Soviet, Afro-Asian,
Asian, African, Arab, Scandinavian, Benelux, European Community,
Western European (and others), and Latin American groups, tend to
have a geographic base. Not all the members of a particular
geographic area, however, may be members of a group or even be
viewed as desireable members. For example, the Union of South
Africa is not a member of the African or Afro-Asian groups. Also,
members from outside a geographic region may meet with a group on
certain matters. For example, the United States and Japan meet
with the Western European (and other) group on economic and legal
matters. In this connection, Canada, Australia, and New Zealand
are regular members of the Western European (an others) group.
The Commonwealth group, without a geographic basis, at one time
was considered a caucusing group, but is no longer considered so

because of the infrequency and informality of its meetings.

Some caucusing groups are groups within larger groups. For example, all of the members of the Arab, African, and Asian groups are members of the Afro-Asian group. (Somewhat earlier, the situation was even more complicated when the Casablanca and Brazzaville groups were subdivisions of the African group and the Casablanca group cut into the membership of the Arab group.) Also, the Scandinavian, European Community, and Benelux groups are subdivisions of the Western European (and others) group. Ignoring such subdivisions, however, four fairly distinct groups emerge, that is: the Soviet, Afro-Asian, Western European, and Latin American groups.

In general, the less economically developed a group's members are, the more supranational their views tend to be concerning caucusing group activity. Thus, members of less developed groups, such as the Arab and Afro-Asian groups, are more likely to see caucusing group activity having impact on their national governments, express a desire to make caucusing group decisions binding, and view caucusing group activity as helping the United Nations more than members of the more developed groups, such as the Western European (and others) and Soviet groups. Also, the meetings of the less developed groups tend to be more frequent and cover a greater range of issues than those of the developed groups.

Although caucusing groups do not make the decisions that are binding upon their members, nevertheless the interaction which goes on between members during meetings helps shape their attitudes toward resolutions and elections. Also, it is not uncommon for a single member of a caucusing group to speak on behalf of the entire group, after a consensus has been reached.

United Nations Delegates and Their Protections

For the United Nations to actually function it was necessary to get some agreement on rules governing represenatives (delegates) sent to the United Nations building in New York. In this connection, a delegate is expected to represent his or her nation's interest in the organization and must present their credentials to a credentials committee and be approved by the General Assembly before they can legally speak or participate in the sessions. Many delegates serve for several sessions and most are housed in permanent missions close to the United Nations building in New York.

Delegates are conceptualized as distinct from the staff of the United Nations itself, such as those composing the Secretariat. The latter are viewed as international civil servants while the former are viewed as biased representatives of their countries. The important meetings of the United Nations, such as those of the General Assembly, Security Council, etc., are composed of and run by delegates, within the latitude allowed by

their home governments. Some governments give considerable
freedom to their delegates who have an important influence on the
shaping of United Nations policies.

Protections for delegates were provided for in the the
Convention on The Privileges and Immunities of the United Nations,
approved by the General Assembly in 1947. The Assembly encouraged
accession by all member states. Among its provisions are ones
providing for: (1) freedom from taxation for the United Nations
and the salaries of United Nations officials, including tax-free
operations of United Nations organs (i.e., UNICEF); (2) travel
rights by UN officials into and out of member states which adhere
to the Convention (through the use of a laissez passer issued by
the United Nations); (3) the right of the United Nations to
contract and initiate legal proceedings; (4) immunity from legal
proceedings against the property and assets of the United Nations;
(5) the inviolability of United Nations property and assets from
search, requisition, confiscation, and expropriation; (6) the
right of the United Nations to hold and deal with assets and
property; (7) freedom from interference and censorship regarding
United Nations publications and communications; and (8) privileges
and immunities for United Nations diplomats and members of the
Secretariat. The bulk of the member states (not including the
United States) have adhered to the Convention. The arrangements
between the United States and the United Nations are specified
instead by a special Headquarters Agreement, which incorporates
most of the above provisions.

Nation Membership in the United Nations

United Nation members are divided into two
classifications--original and subsequent.

Original members are United Nations members which ratified
the United Nations Charter after signing the United Nations
Declaration and/or after participating in the San Francisco
Conference. (Poland is the only original member which did not
participate in the Conference.) Other states are designated as
subsequent members and must meet Charter qualifications and be
brought in through certain procedures. The original members are:
Argentina, Australia, Belgium, Bolivia, Brazil, Byelorussian
S.S.R., Canada, Chile, China, Colombia, Costa Rica, Cuba,
Czechoslovakia, Denmark, Dominican Republic, Ecuador, El Salvador,
Ethiopia, France, Greece, Guatemala, Haiti, Honduras, India, Iran,
Iraq, Lebanon, Liberia, Luxembourg, Mexico, Netherlands, New
Zealand, Nicaragua, Norway, Panama, Paraguay, Peru, Philipines,
Poland, Saudi Arabia, Turkey, Ukranian S.S.R., Union of South
Africa, Egypt (United Arab Republic), Union of Soviet Socialist
Republics, United Kingdom, United States, Uruguay, Venezuela, and
Yugoslavia.

Four of the above---India, Philippines, Ukranian S.S.R., and
Byelorussian S.S.R.---were not states when they became members,

although India and the Philippines have since become states. This is true despite the Charter which maintains "The original Members. . .shall be states" (Chapter II, Article 3). Technically, only forty-nine of the original members are presently states while two of them are subdivisions of one state---the USSR. This stands in contrast to the legal status of subsequent members, all of which have been and presently are states.

As noted, all members of the United Nations which are not original members are classified as "subsequent members." Article 4 of the Charter opens the organization to "all other peace-loving states which accept the obligations contained in the present Charter and in the judgment of the Organization are able and willing to carry out these obligations." Procedurally, the Security Council recommends (veto applies) and the General Assembly decides (two-thirds majority) upon membership. Conflicts in the Security Council in the post-war period between East and West over their respective candidates i.e., Italy (West),Bulgaria (East) led to a partial deadlock in the Security Council over admissions, preventing the Security Council from making recommendations to the General Assembly concerning membership for a number of states. It became clear that criteria other than those specified in the Charter were being applied in some cases. After a request from the General Assembly, the International Court of Justice gave an advisory opinion on the subject in 1948, maintaining, in effect, that only the Charter criteria should apply and that it would be improper to make approval of one state contingent upon the approval of another state. Thus, presumably, each state was to be admitted on its own merits if it met Charter requirements. Regardless of this opinion, however, the deadlock persisted. In view of this, the General Assembly asked the Court whether it would be proper for the General Assembly to admit states on its own. The Court replied, in effect, in an advisory opinion in 1950, that the Security Council recommendation was an essential prerequisite in the admissions process. The deadlock over admissions was broken in 1955 when the Security Council recommended to admit sixteen states, after a bargain to link the admission together, despite the earlier Court opinion. Since that time virtually all states wishing to gain admission have been able to do so. Certain important entities, however, do remain outside the organization. These are: Switzerland, Republic of Korea (South), Democratic People's Republic of Korea (North) and Taiwan. Switzerland's, nonmembership is an expression of her "neutrality." The Koreas and Taiwan have partially clouded legal existences relating to partition which are basically a product of the cold war or wars in Asia.

Previously, East and West Germany were excluded for similar reasons. On June 12, 1973, however, East Germany applied for admission, followed by West Germany. The Security Council recommended on June 22, 1973, that both Germanies be admitted as the 133rd and 134th members of the United Nations. This was generally considered an indication that the United Nations was moving toward virtually universal membership.

Dominica entered the UN as its 151st member in December, 1978.

Membership carries with it normal privileges unless the General Assembly and Security Council decide to sanction a state through suspension or explusion. In the former case, a member of the United Nations may have its rights of membership suspended by the General Assembly (two-thirds vote) upon the recommendation of the Security Council (veto applies). Presumably, suspension is evoked only when "preventive or enforcement action has been taken by the Security Council" (Article 5). Restoration of suspended rights is determined by the Security Council alone. Thus far, no state has had its rights of membership suspended.

Even harsher, a state may be expelled from the United Nations by the General Assembly (two-thirds vote) upon the recommendation of the Security Council (veto applies). Presumably, expulsion occurs only when a state "has persistently violated the principles contained in the present Charter" (Article 6). If readmission is sought after expulsion, presumably, all of the provisions concerning subsequent members apply. Until readmission, an expelled member holds the same status as a nonmember. That is, certain Charter provisions are still binding upon it. Thus far, no state has been expelled from the United Nations.

For a nation's delegates to be seated, however, they must pass review by the Credentials Committee, a procedural committee of the General Assembly, consisting of nine members recommended by the President of the General Assembly and appointed by the General Assembly. Procedurally, delegates submit their credentials to the Secretariat which, after an investigation, submits a report to the Credentials Committee which, in turn, reports to the General Assembly. The latter makes a final determination on credential matters. Through this procedure, the General Assembly decides which delegates can legally speak and participate on behalf of their member states in the Assembly. For example, in October, 1973, the United Nations General Assembly refused by a vote of 72 to 37, to accept South Africa's credentials as a symbolic protest of its racist apartheid policies.

The Charter of the United Nations does not mention the question of or procedures for withdrawal from the organization. It is generally assumed that each state has the exclusive right to make such a determination. Indonesia is the only state to have exercised this right (January, 1965) and did so in the face of requests not to do so, including that of the Secretary-General. In September, 1966, Indonesia rejoined the organization.

Assessments of Members

All members are expected to pay a fair share in the costs of the organization.

The Committee on Contributions, an eighteen-member standing

committee of the General Assembly, functions to advise the Assembly on the apportionment of United Nations expenses among the members. Members of the committee are appointed by the Assembly, using geographic and merit considerations, for three-year terms with immediate eligibility for reappointment, although no two members can be nationals of the same member state. The scale of assessments formulated by the Committee and accepted by the Assembly is based on ability to pay, defined in terms of national income. Once a scale is adopted by the General Assembly, it remains effective for a three-year period unless serious factors arise, recognized by the General Assembly, which disturb a state's ability to pay.

An important question on assessments arose after special assessments were levied to pay for General Assembly peace-keeping operations in the Suez and Congo crises. Are member states obligated to pay these costs, as they are in the case of regular assessments? The International Court of Justice was asked to give an advisory opinion on the subject in 1961, and the Court replied (July, 1962) that special assessments for peace-keeping operations by the General Assembly were to be paid by member states like regular assessments. Several states, however, ignored the advice of the Court on this matter. The General Assembly attempted to alleviate its financial situation by voting in 1961 to sell $200,000,000 worth of twenty-five year bonds to member states. Presumably, the bonds were to be paid off through regular assessments. A number of states, however, refused to pay that portion of their assessments which were to be used to retire the bonds (i.e., USSR, France). Various efforts were then made to solicit funds on a purely voluntary basis to take care of financial obligations not met by regular assessments.

An important principle, revising the assessment situation, was established when the General Assembly voted on December 15, 1972, to limit the maximum contribution of any single member state to 25% of the United Nations budget. This resolution reduced the United States' contribution by approximately $13 million. The Assembly further approved a resolution to request the Contributions Committee to take into account the world economic conditions in the calculation of the rate of assessment of the low-per-capita-income countries, adjusting the minimum rate of assessment from 0.04% to 0.02%, The 1978-1979 budget totalled $1,090,113,500, excluding trust funds and special contributions, and the costs of specialized organizations. The US contributed 25%; the USSR, 11.6%; Japan, 8.64%; West Germany, 7.7%; France, 5.82%; China, 5.5%; and Great Britain, 4.52%. Since 1945 the US has spent over $25 billion dollars on the United Nations, including its financial institutions.

Major Organs of the United Nations

Article 7 of the Charter of the United Nations establishes the General Asembly, Security Council, Economic and Social Council, Trusteeship Council, International Court of Justice, and Secretariat as principal organs. All other organs are designated as specialized or subsidiary, and such distinctions are important for the operations and powers of the organs. In terms of actual relationships, however, the Security Council, General Assembly, and International Court of Justice may be viewed as relatively autonomous coequals, while the Economic and Social Council and Trusteeship Council operate, basically, under the General Assembly. The Secretariat combines the characteristics of partial automony and partial subservience relative to the other principal organs.

THE GENERAL ASSEMBLY

The General Assembly is designated as a principal organ by the Charter of the United Nations (Article 7). Superficially, it appears to be coequal with the other principal organs. In fact, however, it is the central organ of the organization, exceeding all others in importance with, perhaps, the exception of the Security Council in certain matters. Each member is represented by five delegates and five alternate delegates; however, each member has only one vote.

The General Assembly's wide ranging responsibilities are made explicit in Chapter IV of the Charter. The most important provision, Article 10, gives the General Assembly the right to "discuss any questions or any matters within the scope of the present Charter or relating to the powers and functions of any organs provided for in the present Charter, and, except as provided in Article 12, may make recommendations to the Members of the United Nations or to the Security Council or to both on any such questions or matters." The General Assembly's right to "recommend," however, stands in contrast to the Security Council's power to "decide" on a number of matters. The qualification referred to in Article 10, regarding the General Assembly's right of recommendation treated in Article 12, concerns a prohibition on the right of the General Assembly to make recommendations in regard to a "dispute or situation unless the Security Council so requests" if the Security Council itself is dealing with the matter. This provision, presumably, makes it impossible for the two organs to work at crosspurposes to one another in respect to disputes or situations. In fact, the General Assembly has, at times, taken up and made recommendations on matters which are on the agenda of the Security Council. This behavior has been justified on the grounds that the Assembly is considering a different aspect of the question than the Security Council. In any case, this provision does not prevent the General Assembly from discussing identical questions but merely limits the General Assembly from making recommendations until the Security Council is no longer seized with the matter.

To facilitate the above provisions, the Secretary-General, "with the consent of the Security Council, shall notify the General Assembly at each session of any matter relative to the maintenance of international peace and security which are being dealt with by the Security Council and shall similarly notify the General Assembly, or the Members of the United Nations if the General Assembly is not in session, immediately after the Security Council ceases to deal with such matters" (Article 12).

Within the above limitations, the right of the General Assembly to make recommendations on collective security matters is clearly affirmed by the second paragraph of Article 11. "The General Assembly may discuss any questions relating to the

maintenance of international peace and security brought before it
by any member of the United Nations, or by the Security Council,
or by a state which is not a Member . . . [and] . . . may make
recommendations with regard to any such question to the state or
states concerned or to the Security Council or to both."

In this connection, however, a question sometimes arises as
to whether the General Assembly may recommend the use of military
force. The last sentence of paragraph 2, Article 11, seems to
cause some confusion. It states "any such question on which
action is necessary shall be referred to the Security Council by
the General Assembly either before or after discussion." If one
interprets this to mean military action, it appears that the
General Assembly is not authorized by the Charter to do more, in
respect to the maintenance of peace and security, than recommend
measures short of force. This has been the Eastern (Communist)
interpretation of this provision and has been one basis for the
rejection of the Uniting for Peace Resolution.

Another responsibility of the General Assembly is to
"consider the general principles of cooperation in the maintenance
of peace and security, including the principles governing
disarmament and the regulation of armaments, and make
recommendations in regard to such principles to the members or to
the Security Council or to both" (Article 11, Par.1). The General
Assembly has exercised this prerogative a number of times,
particularly in respect to the problem of disarmament; the most
notable case being the General Assembly's acceptance of a version
of the Baruch Plan to guide the work of the Atomic Energy
Commission.

The General Assembly is also directed to initiate studies,
make recommendations, and foster cooperation in respect to
international law, human rights, and fundamental freedoms; and in
the political, economic, social, cultural, educational, and health
fields (Article 13). One limitation put on the General Assembly
in respect to its studies and recommendations concerning these
matters is they must be "without distinction as to race, sex,
language, or religion" (Article 13, Par. 2)

The General Assembly has frequently used the human rights
portions of the Charter to attempt to influence state behavior.
For example, a 1977 General Assembly promoted conference in
Nigeria condemned the South African practice of apartheid as a
violation of the Charter.

The General Assembly is also empowered to make
recommendations of peaceful settlement in respect to situations
detrimental to the general welfare and friendly relations of
states and situations arising from the "violation of the
provisions of the present Charter" (Article 14). These
provisions, again, seem to imply that the General Assembly should
be basically concerned with recommending peaceful adjustments
rather than with the employment of force to maintain peace and
security. The General Assembly has also attempted to affect state

behavior, in terms of such provisions, as in the case of
condemning any state support of hijacking (1977) in the
international system.

The pivotal position of the General Assembly is emphasized in
Article 15, which requires that the other organs of the United
Nations report to it. (The General Assembly on the other hand,
does not report to any other organ.) In the case of the Security
Council, the reports must "include an account of the measures that
the Security Council has decided upon or taken to maintain
international peace and security." One might think that such
provisions would open the door to General Assembly scrutiny of
Security Council activities; typically, however, the Security
Council's report is accepted without discussion.

The General Assembly's concern with the international
trusteeship system (detailed provisions are specified in Chapters
XII and XIII) is established in Article 16 and the Assembly must
approve "the trusteeship agreements for the areas not designated
as strategic." In contrast, strategic trust arrangements are
approved by the Security Council. At present, there is only one
remaining trust territory, the Pacific Islands, administered by
the United States. There are four island groups in the Trust
Territory. In January, 1978, the Northern Marianas voted to
become, like Puerto Rico, a US commonwealth. In July of that same
year, the three remaining island groups began drafting a
constitution to become a new nation—the Federated States of
Micronesia. Independence is expected sometime in 1981.

Other provisions, in Chapter IV treat the budget, voting,
sessions, rules of procedure, and the right of the Assembly to
create subsidiary organs.

Generally speaking, the General Assembly has vigorously
expanded its role and functions over time, almost, at times, to
the point of jeopardizing the United Nations, because of the
financial obligations incurred.

The General Assembly meets every year starting on the third
Tuesday in September until a closing date set by the Assembly upon
the recommendation of the General Committee. Meetings normally
take place at the Headquarters in New York, although a majority of
members can establish some other meeting place. The first regular
session was held in London on January 10-February 14, 1946 and in
New York on October 23-December 16, 1946.

For a time the General Assembly met on a continuous basis
because the Security Council did not function as planned. This
was done through the device of the Interim Committee, consisting
of all member states, created in November of 1947. The Interim
Committee made some recommendations and conducted some studies
when it was active. One, for example, concerned the use of the
veto power in the Security Council. Its real reason for existence
was eliminated by the Uniting for Peace Resolution of 1950 and it
adjourned sine die in 1955.

Much attention is paid to agenda construction prior to actual meetings. In line with this a provisional agenda is drawn up by the Secretary General and distributed to member states sixty days prior to the opening session. It includes: (1) reports from the Secretary-General and organs of the United Nations, including many of the specialized agencies; (2) items proposed by member states (nonmember states under certain conditions), principal organs, or the Secretary-General; and (3) budgetary items. The provisional agenda is scrutinized by the General Committee (treated below). Also, member states, principal organs, and the Secretary-General may, at least thirty days prior to the regular session, place agenda items on a supplementary list, to be considered along with the provisional agenda. The supplementary list must be circulated to members at least twenty days before the session. In the case of special sessions, however, such items may be placed up to four days prior to the session and are circulated as soon as possible.

Also, additional items can be added to the agenda by a simple majority of General Assembly members during such sessions.

The final agenda is approved in plenary sessions. Plenary sessions are meetings of all members which speak and act officially in the name of the General Assembly. Thus, recommendations and resolutions adopted in plenary sessions have the authority of the General Assembly behind them; while matters considered and adopted in the main committees and other bodies are work preparatory to consideration in the plenary sessions. In addition, important elections (i.e., those of the nonpermanent members of the Security Council and judges of the International Court of Justice) and the General Debate take place in plenary sessions.

Occasionally, special sessions are held. A special session is a meeting of the Assembly at some time other than during its regular meeting period. Such sessions may be requested by: (1) a procedural vote of the Security Council; (2) a majority of United Nations members; or (3) a single member of the United Nations if a majority of members concur within thirty days after notification is sent to the Secretary-General. Meetings are to be held within fifteen days of a legitimate request. Special Sessions have been held on Palestine in 1947, 1948, 1963, and 1967; on Lebanon in 1958; on the Congo in 1960; on South Africa and the Middle East in 1967; on raw materials in 1974; on International Economic Cooperation in 1975; and on Namibia and Disarmament in 1978. The 1975 Special Session was notable because it focused on accelerating the progress of developing nations and on closing the gap between developed and developing nations.

Closely related to special sessions are emergency special sessions which are called in the same way as special sessions but are held within twenty-four hours instead of fifteen days of the time of a legitimate request. Unless the General Assembly decides otherwise, the item relating to the emergency is immediately taken up in plenary session, without prior reference to the General Committee or a main committee. In short, emergency special sessions deal with matters so serious that they permit no procedural delay.

The President, Vice-Presidents, and General Committee

The President is the principal, elected officer of the General Assembly. He serves for the session during which he was elected (including special and emergency sessions) and exercises the following functions: (1) opens and closes, through declaration, plenary meetings and (2) directs discussion in plenary meetings with the power to (a) accord the right to speak (always granted), (b) put the question, (c) announce decisions, (d) rule on points of order (may be overruled by the General Assembly), (e) maintain order, (f) propose time and frequency limits on speakers, (g) propose closure on speakers, (h) propose suspension or adjournment of the meeting, and (i) propose adjournment of debate.

The President is a member of and automatically presides over the General Committee (treated below).

In general, the President is an important influence on the course of events in the General Assembly but remains under the authority of the Assembly. If it is necessary for a President to be absent from a meeting he appoints a Vice-President in his place who assumes, as acting President, his powers. If a President resigns or is unable to function, a new President is elected. The past President or the chairman of his state's delegation serves at each new session until a successor is elected.

The office of the President is viewed as a "small power" privilege; that is, Presidents are drawn from states other than the five permanent members of the Security Council.

At the beginning of each regular session the General Assembly also elects seventeen Vice-Presidents who have the primary function of serving on the General Committee. In the interest of geographical balance and other factors, Vice-Presidents are allocated according to the following formula: seven to African and Asian states, one to an Eastern European state, three to Latin American states, two to Western European and other states, and one to each of the permanent members of the Security Council with the proviso that the election of the President from one of these regions will have the effect of reducing, by one, the number of Vice-Presidencies allocated to it. (Allocation of Vice-President positions to the Big Five stands in contrast to the fact that they never obtain chairmanships of Main Committees).

The President, Vice-President, and Chairmen of the main committees constitute the General Committee. The General Committee is authorized to: (1) review the provisional agenda and make recommendations to the General Assembly; (2) assist the President of the General Assembly in his work; (3) review the progress of the General Assembly; and (4) recommend a closing date for the General Assembly session. Some of these functions have been superseded by informal means (i.e., luncheon meetings).

General Procedures

General Debate occurs at the beginning of each annual session. It consists of a series of speeches, given by delegates wishing to speak, ranging over a wide variety of topics. These speeches tend to stand in contrast to the focus on agenda items taking place in the main committees.

When in plenary session, all items treated by the General Assembly are divided into "important" and "other" categories. Article 18 of the Charter specifies important questions as:

recommendations with respect to the maintenance of international peace and security, the election of the non-permanent members of the Security Council, the election of the members of the Economic and Social Council, the election of members of the Trusteeship Council . . . the admission of new Members to the United Nations, the suspension of the rights and privileges of membership, the expulsion of Members, questions relating to the operation of the trusteeship system, and budgetary questions.

Questions not listed automatically fall into the "other" category. However, questions can be moved to the "important" category by a simple majority vote.

"Important" questions are decided by a two-thirds majority and "other" questions by a simple majority. In both cases, ratios are determined by the number of members present and voting. Thus a large number of abstentions will not prevent a passing vote if the proper ratio and a quorum (majority of members) is met.

Although procedural votes in the General Assembly are normally taken through a show of hands, any state has the right to request a roll call vote on any matter. The roll call vote is taken in the English alphabetical order of the names of member states beginning with the member state's name drawn by the President of the Assembly. When a member state is called its representative is required to reply "yes," "no," or "abstention."

Main Committees

There are seven main committees in the General Assembly. These are: (1) Political and Security Committee; (1a) Special Political Committee; (2) Economic and Financial Committee; (3) Social, Humanitarian and Cultural Committee; (4) Decolonization Committee; (5) Administrative and Budgetary Committee; (6) Legal Committee. Each member state is represented on each committee and exercises one vote. A simple majority voting system is used, with one-third of the membership constituting a quorum; although, at least a majority of the members must be present during voting. The main work of the committees is the discussion of agenda items and the preparation of draft resolutions for plenary sessions.

Much of the work is facilitated through the use of subcommittees. Each main committee elects its own officers, which are the chairman, vice-chairman, and rapporteur. The chairmanship is recognized as a medium and small power (other than the Big Five) privilege to offset large power dominance elsewhere in the United Nations. The officer positions are distributed geographically and based on merit.

The Political and Security Committee (The First) handles agenda items such as those relating to peace and security, disarmament, pacific settlement, and the admission, suspension, and expulsion of members.

The Special Political Committee shares the work of the Political and Security Committee. Because the latter committee was overburdened, an Ad Hoc Political Committee was established to help it during the second session of the General Assembly. This committee was reestablished on a yearly basis until 1956 when it was made permanent and renamed the Special Political Committee.

The Economic and Financial Committee (The Second) deals with problems and questions implied by its name. This includes concern with the Economic and Social Council and specialized agencies. Its focus upon the broader aspects of world economic developments and standards of living may be contrasted to the more technical work of the Administrative and Budgetary Committee. The Charter on the Economic Rights and Duties of States, adopted by the General Assembly in 1974, stemmed from the work of this committee.

The Social, Humanitarian, and Cultural Committee (The Third) is concerned with the problems and questions implied by its name, particularly in connection with the Economic and Social Council and specialized agencies.

The Trusteeship Committee (The Fourth) deals with questions and problems connected with the Trusteeship Council as well as non-self-governing territories which are not part of the trusteeship system.

The Administrative and Budgetary Committee (The Fifth) handles United Nations budgetary questions, including those of specialized agencies, as well as administrative questions relating to the Secretariat.

The Legal Committee (the Sixth) is concerned with the development of international law and legal questions. The more technical formulations of international law (drafting and codification) are handled by the International Law Commission.

Additional Historically Notable Committees and Other Bodies of the General Assembly

Historically important committees and other bodies that have facilitated the work of the General Assembly include: the Advisory Committee on Administrative and Budgetary Questions, Atomic Energy Commission, International Atomic Energy Agency, International Refugee Organization, Committee on Non-Self-Governing Territories,

Disarmament Commission, Special Committee, International Law
Commission, Committee on the Peaceful Uses of Outer Space, United
Nations Children's Fund, and United Nations Emergency Force.

Advisory Committee on Administrative and Budgetary Questions

The Advisory Committee on Administrative and Budgetary
Questions is a sixteen-member, standing committee of the General
Assembly which reviews the Secretary-General's budget estimates
and budgetary matters in connnection with the specialized
agencies, and reports to and assists the Administrative and
Budgetary Committee. Committee members are appointed for
three-year terms by the General Assembly and are selected on a
geographic basis and for personal qualifications and experience.
At least two committee members must be recognized financial
experts, and no two members can be nationals of the same state.

International Atomic Energy Agency Atomic Energy Commission

The Atomic Energy Commission was created by the General
Assembly in January, 1946, to work out a plan for the control of
atomic energy. During its life, the Commission reported to the
Security Council and was composed of the members of the Security
Council plus Canada. Although the General Assembly endorsed the
Baruch Plan to guide the Commission in respect to the control of
atomic energy, the USSR offered alternative plans. This led to a
deadlock in the Commission by 1948. The principal points of
disagreement included: (1) the question of the veto applying in
Security Council decisions relating to the Commission's work; (2)
the problem of the kind and extent of inspection and controls; and
(3) the question of national vs. international ownership. In
general, the Soviet Union opposed the supranational character of
the Western proposals (i.e., the USSR wanted the veto, more
limited inspection, and national ownership). AEC was disbanded in
1952 with the formation of the Disarmament Commission.

International Atomic Energy Agency

The International Atomic Energy Agency came into existence on
July 29, 1957, after twenty-six states ratified the statute
establishing the organization. This followed an address by
President Eisenhower in 1953 which stressed the need to establish
an international agency to further the peaceful uses of atomic
energy. The General Assembly unanimously adopted a resolution to
establish such an agency in 1954. An international
conference---which followed in September, 1956, attended by
eighty-one states---unanimously adopted the statute providing for
the structure and functions of the organization.

Although related to the United Nations through a special
agreement, IAEA is not viewed as a specialized agency. Under the

terms of the United Nations agreement, IAEA reports annually to the General Assembly and the latter may make recommendations in respect to the IAEA regular budget. IAEA has the right, when appropriate, to report to the Economic and Social Council and, if necessary, to the Security Council concerning violations of IAEA regulations relating to the peaceful uses of nuclear material. (Specialized agencies, in contrast, report to and come to an agreement only with the Economic and Social Council.)

The basic purpose of IAEA is to promote the peaceful uses of atomic energy. To further this purpose, IAEA gathers and disseminates technical information, particularly helping less technically advanced nations; facilitates the flow of nuclear materials to those states needing them, by arranging sales and purchases; provides technical assistance with respect to nuclear programs; engages in training and research activity, including the granting of fellowships and the development of non-military uses of nuclear power; organizes and sponsors technical conferences; conducts studies to facilitate the use of nuclear materials; fosters safety standards; and attempts to safeguard against the diversion of nuclear materials to military uses.

To further this latter function, the agency has obtained the right of inspection in respect to certain nuclear facilities made available through the Agency. Even in those cases where non-IAEA arranged (bilateral) negotiations have led to the establishment of nuclear facilities, however, the nations involved may request IAEA administration of nuclear safeguards. This was the case, for example, in respect to bilateral facilities agreements between the United States, on the one hand, and Argentina, Austria, China, Greece, Iran, Norway, Philipines, Portugal, Thailand, Indonesia, and South Vietnam on the other. Also, one of the conditions of US nuclear aid to Indonesia (January, 1966), in respect to the Atoms for Peace Program, was to give IAEA inspection rights to insure that the US donated reactor be used only for peaceful, nonmilitary purposes.

There has been considerable pressure to make such practices universal. William G. Foster, in addressing the eighteen-nation United Nations Disarmament Committee in Geneva on January 27, 1966, argued:

> we must continue to secure application of international atomic agency or equivalent international safeguards over peaceful nuclear activities . . . I urge agreement that all transfers of nuclear materials or equipment for peaceful purposes to countries which do not have nuclear weapons be under IAEA, or equivalent international safeguards.

To facilitate its work, the Agency contacts and works with other agencies dealing in the atomic area---for example, regional ones like Euratom. IAEA maintains a library and is responsible for numerous publications including Nuclear Fission (bimonthly), Atomic Energy Review (quarterly), the IAEA Bulletin (bimonthly) and Automindex (monthly). The major organs of IAEA are the

General Conference, the Board of Governors, and the
Director-General.

Each member state of the organization is a member of the
General Conference which meets yearly in Vienna. Each member
possesses one vote, and a simple majority suffices on all
questions except those concerning: the suspension of a member;
financial questions; the adoption of amendments; and financial
questions, where a two-thirds majority is required. The
Conference functions to review the work of the Board of Governors,
approve the budget, and approve the reports to the United Nations.
The Conference can make recommendations to the Board of Governors
and to member states individually. In practice, the Conference
takes a secondary role to the Board of Governors. Special
Sessions of the Conference may be convened upon the request of a
majority of member states or the Board of Governors.

The Board of Governors, consisting of representatives from
thirty-four states, has primary authority and responsibility to
carry out the various functions of the organization. The majority
of the members of the Board are appointed by a previous Board,
according to various criteria. For example, the states most
advanced in their atomic technology; the United States, Canada,
the United Kingdom, the USSR, and France, are always members of
the Board. Certain states which represent the most advanced
technology on a regional basis; such as Australia, India, Japan,
and Brazil, also, as long as they continue their leadership
position, remain members of the Board. Other states are named
because they are primary producers of nuclear materials or
suppliers of technical assistance. The remaining members of the
Board are elected by majority vote by the General Conference with
due regard to regional representation. Most decisions of the
Board require a simple majority vote, although budgetary matters
and appointment of the Director-General require a two-thirds
majority. The Board meets upon the request of a member state, the
Director-General, the General Conference, or on its own
initiative. Typically, it meets four times a year at the
headquarters in Vienna. In practice, the Board is the central hub
of the organization, overshadowing both the Director-General and
tne General Conference.

The Director-General heads the Secretariat of IAEA in Vienna
and operates under the supervision of the Board of Governors. He
is appointed for a four-year term by the Board of Governors
(two-thirds vote) upon the approval of the General Conference
(majority vote). Members of the Secretariat, numbering
approximately 1,250, are recruited principally for their
efficiency and technical competence with due regard for geographic
distribution. More than half of the member states have nationals
serving on the Secretariat. Under the guidance of the
Director-General, the members of the staff are involved in the
numerous assistance, information, and research functions of the
organization.

Regular budget expenses recommended by the Board of Governors and approved by the General Conference are borne by the member states, and assessed according to ability to pay. In addition, voluntary contributions comprise a general fund used for various operational activities. The 1979 budget was set at $65,177,000. The organization also receives monies for its role in the United Nations Development Program.

Any state recommended by the Board of Governors and approved by the General Conference (majority vote) may become a member of the organization. Members of the United Nations and the specialized agencies were given membership simply by ratification if this occurred within ninety days after approval of the organization's statutes in 1956. There are 110 members, including the Communist states which belong to the United Nations.

International Refugee Organization

The International Refugee Organization was established in 1946 by the General Assembly as a temporary, specialized agency of the United Nations, after a recommendation to establish such an agency by the Economic and Social Council. IRO took over from the United Nations Relief and Rehabilitation Agency (abolished in December of 1946) the problem of alleviating the plight of World War II refugees. Until its demise in January, 1952, IRO processed over one million refugees, and its functions included camp maintenance, the supply of food and medical equipment, training and orientation, transportation, facilitation of repatriation, tracing services (to reunite families), and foster home placement. Most of those resettled were accepted by the United States, Australia, and New Zealand. Communist countries were opposed to the basic principles guiding IRO, particularly IRO's inclusion of "enemy" persons as refugees, and the practice of allowing refugees the right to refuse repatriation. For these and other reasons, UNited Nations Communist states voted against the establishment of IRO. The major participants and contributors to IRO were non-Communist states---i.e., Australia, Belgium, Canada, China, France, Italy, Norway, and the United States. Policy for IRO was established by a General Council (all member states) and carried out by a Director-General and an Executive Committee (nine states). Contributions and expenditures to IRO exceeded $400 million, roughly half of which was used for transportation to receiving states.

Committee on Non-Self-Governing Territories

The Committee on Information from Non-Self-Governing Territories was created in 1947 by the Assembly to examine required reports on non-self-governing territories. The Committee was divided equally between states submitting reports and those not submitting reports with the latter elected for three-year

terms by the Trusteeship Committee (The Fourth) of the Assembly.
Procedurally, the reports passed first to the Department of
Trusteeship and Non-Self-Governing Territories in the Secretariat,
where the information was analyzed, and then to the Committee
which, after due consideration, made recommendations to the
Assembly concerning the territories, on both procedural and
substantive matters, in the economic, social and educational
fields. On December 16, 1963, the Committee was dissolved by the
General Assembly and its functions taken over by the Special
Committee.

Disarmament Commission

The General Assembly created the Disarmament Commission in
January, 1952, after an address by President Truman to the
Assembly in 1950 on the desirability of merging the work of the
Commission for Conventional Armaments and the Atomic Energy
Commission. The new Commission, therefore, considers all phases
of disarmament, in contrast to the previous division of labor
between the atomic and conventional commissions. The members of
the Disarmament Commission, initially were members of the Security
Council plus Canada. It was charged with formulating plans that
would incorporate an international control organ, verification and
disclosure schemes, and a system of safeguards. As in the case of
the two previous commissions, however, disagreements between East
and West continued upon basically the same lines. That is, the
West tended to stress the need for inspection and control while
the USSR and its allies stressed the need to illegalize nuclear
weapons and dismantle foreign bases. After initial focus upon a
general plan of disarmament and possible force level freezes in
the arms race, discussions tended to center more and more upon
disclosure and possible warning systems against surprise attack.
Discussions also included the possibility of creating aerial
inspection zones within the USSR, Europe, and the United States.
In 1958, the Commission was expanded to include all United Nations
members, but, since that time, it has been eclipsed by other
disarmament developments, both inside and outside the United
Nations.

Special Committee

The Special Committee on the Ending of Colonialism was
created in 1961 by the General Assembly to facilitate the
implementation of the Assembly's Declaration on the Granting of
Independence to Colonial Countries and Peoples. The Committee's
members reflect a geographic balance and are nominated by the
President of the General Assembly. Also known as the Committee on
Decolonization, its 24 members see their goal as the banning of
colonialism which they define as racism, apartheid, foreign
economic exploitation and the waging of colonial wars. The

Committee sends missions to visit colonial peoples in order to
study their living conditions. Since its inception it has been
credited with facilitating the emergence of 70 million people from
dependent status.

International Law Commission

The International Law Commission was created by the General
Assembly in November, 1947. It originally consisted of fifteen
legal experts, elected for five-year terms. Since that time, the
Commission has been expanded to twenty-five mebers. Commission
members are nominated by United Nations members and elected by the
General Assembly with the stipulation that no two members be of
the same nationality and that they represent the main forms of
civilization and the major legal systems of the world. Because
the Commission members function as experts they may not receive
instructions from states concerning their work. Their primary
task is to develop and to codify international law. This does not
mean that the Commission can create international law; rather, the
Commission attempts to draft what it considers to be the essence
of international practice. A typical codification cycle is for
draft codes to go from the Commission to the General Assembly for
approval; to states, for commentary; back to the Commission; to
the General Assembly; and, finally, to an international conference
for adoption. For example, this was the basic cycle in regard to
the United Nations Conference on Diplomatic Intercourse and
Immunities held in Vienna in March-April, 1961, leading to the
adoption of the Vienna Convention on Diplomatic Relations.
The basic direction of the Commission's work was established
by its first session in 1949, when it listed various areas subject
to codification---including the law of treaties, arbitral
procedures, counselor intercourse and immunities, succession of
states and governments, statelessness, and state responsibilities.
Considerable progress has been made in these areas and others, in
the sense that the COmmission has produced a number of draft codes
and made numerous recommendations to the General Assembly.
In addition to this work, the Commission may produce draft
declarations which have a bearing upon international law but which
do not constitute international law. In this category is the
Commission's Draft Declaration of Rights and Duties of States,
prepared in 1949. The Declaration includes such state rights as
independence and equality. The General Assembly has brought this
Declaration to the attention of member states and jurists.
The Commission has also enunciated principles in connection
with the Nuremberg Judgments (by asserting that persons may be
responsible for illegal acts under international law that are not
illegal under national law) and by defining as punishable under
international law crimes against the peace, war crimes, and crimes
against humanity.
However, until such declarations and enunciations of

principles are accepted in international conventions their moral
character is more evident than their legal character.

The Commission's work is summarized in the Yearbook of the
International Law Commission. Other information, of a documentary
character, can be found in the Official Records of particular
sessions. The Commission normally meets annually in Geneva from
three to four months.

Committee on the Peaceful Uses of Outer Space

The Committee on the Peaceful Uses of Outer Space was formed
by the General Assembly in 1959 by expanding the Ad Hoc Committee
of Eighteen. Since then disputes between East and West, similar
to those which have existed in the Disarmament Commission and the
Committee on Disarmament, have hampered the Committee's work. In
1965, however, the Committee was able to issue a Declaration,
approved by the General Assembly, which stressed: (1) the freedom
of states to explore outer space; (2) the extension of
international law to outer space; (3) the need for cooperation
between states engaging in exploration of the same areas; (4) the
application of each state's jurisdiction to its own space
vehicles; and (5) the need for all states to cooperate and to give
assistance to states engaged in space exploration, particularly in
cases of emergency landings and similar situations. These
concepts have been incorporated into the "Treaty on Principles
Governing the Activities of States in the Exploration and Use of
Outer Space, Including the Moon and Other Celestial Bodies."
Also, the Committee signed the "Agreement on the Rescue of
Astronauts, the Return of Astronauts and the Return of Objects
Launched into Outer Space," which went into effect in 1968. Since
then its most significant work has been the completion of the
Convention on International Liability for Damage Caused by Space
Objects, which had been on the Committee's agenda since 1964. It
was adopted in 1972.

United Nations International Children's Fund

The United Nations International Children's Emergency Fund was
created by the General Assembly, in December, 1946, to provide
emergency relief to children because of conditions resulting from
World War II. This mission, continued until 1950, resulted in a
flow of food, medical supplies, and clothing to needy children.
With post-war reconstruction basically accomplished, the General
Assembly broadened the functions of UNICEF and focused its
activities upon the children of underdeveloped areas. In 1953,
the organization's name was changed to the United Nations Children's Fund and established on a permanent basis, although the
UNICEF abbreviation remained the same. Since that time, the Fund
has focused on stimulating projects in health, welfare, disease,
nutrition, education, and vocational training.

Administration is accomplished by an Executive Board and Executive Director.

The Executive Board consists of thirty members, ten of which are elected each year by the Economic and Social Council from members of the specialized agencies and the United Nations. Its function is to establish policy in respect to UNICEF activities and to allocate fund monies for those projects the Board has decided to support.

The Executive Director is appointed by the Secretary-General of the United Nations after consultation with the Executive Board. The Executive Director administers the Fund and directs the UNICEF staff according to the policies established by the Executive Board. The Director reports annually to ECOSOC and that organ takes note of the report and may use the occasion to make recommendations concerning UNICEF activities.

Unlike a specialized agency which typically receives its income from member states according to a scale of contributions relating to a budget, UNICEF operates completely through voluntary contributions and the sale of greeting cards. Contributions are received from governments, private organizations, and private persons. The number of governments contributing has constantly increased so that almost every government makes some contribution. Expenditures for health and education accounted for the majority of funds allocated in 1977. Allocations totalled $142,000,000 for that year, and the organization had commitments of $63,900,000. The Central Headquarters are located in New York with regional and field offices scattered throughout the world. UNICEF publishes a newsletter and various papers of consultative nature.

United Nations Emergency Force

Stemming from the involvement of the General Assembly in Uniting for Peace crises situations, the United Nations Emergency Force was established by a General Assembly resolution of November 5, 1956, to supervise the cessation of hostilities extending from the Suez Canal to armistice demarcation lines established between Egypt and Israel. The creation of the force followed an Israeli invasion of the Sinai Peninsula of Egypt on October 29, 1956, and subsequent French and British military action against Egypt. After consideration and deadlock in the Security Council concerning the Suez situation, the matter passed by the Uniting for Peace Resolution to the General Assembly, and the Secretary-General was requested to draw plans for a supervisory force. After a plan was adopted, the force was constituted and became operational on November 15, 1956. The Secretary-General and a seven-nation advisory committee were given primary responsibility for directing the force, which quickly grew to approximately 6000 men at a cost of about $40,000 per day. Ten states---Brazil, Canada, Colombia, Denmark, Finland, India, Indonesia, Norway, Sweden, and Yugoslavia---supplied military contingents while a number of other

states assisted by supplying medical equipment, food, and other
materials. Although the General Assembly attempted to finance a
sizeable portion of the operation by applying the scale used in
connection with regular assessments, certain states objected and
refused to pay any assessments connected with the Emergency Force.

Special Declarations, Programs, Resolutions and Conferences

Additional historically important aspects of the work of the
General Assembly include: the Universal Declaration of Human
Rights, United Nations Development Program, OPEX Program, Uniting
for Peace Resolution and International Conference on Environment.

Universal Declaration of Human Rights

The General Assembly adopted the Universal Declaration of
Human Rights on December 10, 1948. The Declaration proclaimed
that "the advent of a world in which human beings shall enjoy
freedom of speech and belief and freedom from fear and want. .
.the highest aspiration of the common people." Its thirty
articles deal with problems of equality at birth of all peoples
and equality before the law; discrimination on the basis of sex,
race, political, religious, or any other belief, national or
social origin, property, birth or other status; slavery; degrading
treatment or cruel punishment; protection against tyranny,
oppression, or arbitrary detention and/or exile, and so forth.
Through the Declaration many related activities have been
fostered, including the Commission on the Status of Women, the
Sub-Commission on Prevention of Discrimination and Protection of
Minorities, the Commission of Human Rights and the Committee on
the Elimination of Racial Discrimination. Due to the work of the
latter committee, the General Assembly on December 21, 1965,
adopted the International Convention on the Elimination of All
Forms of Racial Discrimination, signed by sixty-five states as of
June, 1972.

United Nations Development Program

In August, 1964, the Economic and Social Council recommended
a consolidation (completed January 1, 1966) of the Special Fund
with the Expanded Program of Technical Assistance, creating a new
"United Nations Development Program." Distinctions between the
two components of the United Nations Development Program were
completely eliminated as of Januray, 1972, when the merger became
effective. The Inter-Agency Consultative Board supplanted both
the Technical Assistance Board of the Expanded Program and the
Consultative Board of the Special Fund, and a Governing Council
replaced the Technical Assistance Committee of the Expanded
Program and Governing Council of the Fund.
The UNDP is headed by a 48-nation Governing Council which

changes one-third of its membership yearly. It is made up of the
Secretary-General of Inter-Agency Consultation Board plus the
heads of all UNDP agencies. All financing is through voluntary
contributions.

The UNDP is the world's largest agency for technical
cooperation. It has $6 trillion invested in projects in over 150
nations and 26 international agencies. It has 6,650 international
experts from nearly 90 countries of which 4,178 are on
fellowships. Its four Regional locations are: Africa, Asia and
the Pacific, Arab States, and Latin America.

UNDP's five project fields include: (1) surveying resource and
industrial potential; (2) stimulating investment; (3) training;
(4) transferring technology and stimulating local technology; and
(5) economic and social planning (especially for the poor).

Organizations affiliated with UNDP include the UN Natural
Resources Revolving Fund, UN Volunteers, the UN Sahelian Office,
and the UN Trust Fund for Colonial Countries and Peoples.

OPEX Program

The Opex Program was initiated by the General Assembly in
1958 and made operational in 1959. The Program provided technical
assistance to states by arranging for the appointment of United
Nations specialized agency officials to the governments desiring
them. Such officials played an advisory role and helped train
state nationals to play the same role after the appointment period
was over. Salaries were paid for by the recipient government and
supplemented by the United Nations. Presently, UN volunteers,
similar to Peace Corps workers, have replaced this program,
working on the local level rather with government officials.

Uniting For Peace Resolution

The Uniting for Peace Resolution was adopted by the General
Assembly on November 3, 1950, during the Korean conflict. The
United States, France, and the United Kingdom led the drive, in
the face of Security Council impotence, to have the General
Assembly recommend collective security measures if the Security
Council was unable to do so because of the use of the veto. The
resolution was adopted over the objections of the USSR and other
COmmunist states which maintained that the Charter, according to
Article 11, paragraph 2, prohibited any organ other than the
Security Council from calling for forceful collective security
measures. The resolution noted the "failure of the Security
Council to discharge its responsibilities on behalf of all the
Member States . . . [and maintained that] . . . such failure does
not deprive the General Assembly of its rights or relieve it of
its rsponsibilities under the Charter in regard to the maintenance
of international peace and security." It then provides that:

if the Security Council, because of lack of unanimity of

the permanent members, fails to exercise its primary
responsibility for the maintenance of international peace and
security in any case where there appears to be a threat to
the peace, breach of the peace, or act of aggression, the
General Assembly shall consider the matter immediately with
the view to making the appropriate recommendations to Members
for collective measures, including in the case of a breach of
the peace or act of aggression the use of armed force when
necessary, to maintain or restore international peace and
security. If not in session at the time, the General
Assembly may meet in emergency session within twenty-four
hours of the request therefor. Such emergency special
session shall be called if requested by the Security Council
on the vote of any seven members or by a majority of the
Members of the United Nations.

Although employed a number of times in serious international
situations since the Korean War---such as during the Suez,
Hungarian, and Congo Crises---controversy has almost always
surrounded the resolution's use. For example, in the Suez crisis
the British and French United Nations representatives maintained
that it was improperly employed because a veto had not actually
occurred on the issue at hand before it was invoked. The USSR
vigorously opposed its use in both the Hungarian and Congo crises
and this opposition, in turn, was related to the USSR's refusal to
pay for special financial assessments levied in connection with
United Nations force deployments made during the resolution's use.
In practice, most states have not maintained national military
elements for emergency use as requested by the resolution and
United Nations forces have been constituted on an ad hoc basis in
crisis situations (such as the Suez, the Congo, and Cyprus
crises).

International Conference on the Environment

Representatives of 113 nations attended the first
international conference on the environment, held in Stockholm
from June 5-16, 1972. The United Nations-sponsored conference
produced several results which have begun to lead to the
institutionalization of environmental management. Among its
accomplishments were the following: the creation of an
Environmental Secretariat within the United Nations charged with
the coordination of environmental activities; the creation of an
Enviromnemtal Fund, to be financed by voluntary contributions
(initial goal for the first five years was $100 million); a formal
recommendation to the International Whaling Commission requesting
the banning of all commercial whaling for a ten-year period;
approval of the Earthwatch Program, to be carried out by the World
Meteorological Association (WMO), in order to monitor pollution
levels and environmental factors from 110 stations around the
world, and endorsement of the World Heritage Trust Convention.

The Convention attempts to protect certain areas of the world "of such unique natural, historical, or cultural value that they are part of the heritage of all mankind." The conference also produced the Endangered Species Convention; a twenty-six point declaration of environmental principles; and recommendations dealing with trade imbalances created by the protection of the environment.

THE SECURITY COUNCIL

The Security Council is designated as a principal organ by
Article 7 of the Charter and specializes in problems involving the
maintenance of peace and security, operating primarily under
Chapters 6 and 7.

The Security Council embodies the principle that the Big Five
are primarily responsible for peace and security but allows this
function to be shared with the nonpermanent members of the
Council. In the League of Nations system the Assembly and the
Council were copartners in respect to problems of peace and
security (Although, initially, there was great power dominance on
the Council). In the United Nations system, on the other hand,
the Charter makes a fairly clear division of labor between the
organs, and the Security Council stands out as the primary organ
of peacekeeping (although the General Assembly is not prohibited
from dealing with matters of aggression). This shift in emphasis
between the two systems may be characterized as a movement away
from the Wilsonian concept of "all the peace-loving nations
against the few aggressors" to a new concept emphasizing great
power perquisites and responsibilities for the collective security
system.

Because it is primarily an organ of emergency, the Security
Council is required by Article 28 to be organized so that it can
function continuously. This stands in contrast to the General
Assembly's temporary existence during its sessions. (However, the
advantage of the Security Council's permanent session has been
undercut somewhat by the fact that the General Assembly now can
come into special, emergency session, within a twenty-four hour
period, under the Uniting for Peace Resolution.

Members of the United Nations "confer on the Security Council
primary responsibility for the maintenance of international peace
and security, and agree that in carrying out its duties and under
this responsibility the Security Council acts in their behalf"
(Charter, Article 24). Further, they "agree to accept and carry
out the decisions of the Security Council in accordance with the
present Charter" (Charter, Article 25). These commitments stand
in contrast to members' rights, under the League of Nations, to
decide for themselves whether the covenant had been violated.

The fundamental assumption behind the successful operation of
the Security Council is harmony among the great powers, in that
each of its permanent members possesses a veto. The failure to
obtain the great power harmony in the post-war world helps to
explain the relative eclipse of the Security Council through most
of its existence, in comparison with the General Assembly. The
most notable shift in the direction of augmenting the General
Assembly's responsibilities, in the supposed area of primary
concern of the Security Council, occured during the Korean War
with the General Assembly's adoption of the Uniting for Peace

Resolution.

The Secretary-General reviews the credentials of
representatives to the Security Council and the Security Council
decides credential matters. Although the Secretariat examines the
credentials of representatives to the General Assembly and reports
to the Credentials Committee, because each organ decides
credential matters for itself, there exists the possibility of a
discrepancy concerning credentials between the two organs. That
is, the existing system makes it possible the Security Council
could accept the credentials of representatives who are not
accepted by the General Assembly or vice versa.

The Security Council can invite members of the United Nations
to participate in Security Council discussions without a vote if
it considers such members' interests especially affected (Article
31). Nonmembers of the organization which are parties to a
dispute may also be invited to participate without a vote under
conditions established by the Security Council. For example,
Communist China was invited to participate in Security Council
discussions early in the Korean War.

The Security Council has been involved in a number of
historically important disputes.

These include: Kashmir (1947), Israel (1948), Korea (1950),
Suez (1956), Lebanon (1958), Congo (1961), Middle East (1967,
1973), Cyprus (1974), Rhodesia (1976), Lebanon (1978), and
Cambodia (1979).

The Council recently approved a Western-sponsored plan for the
independence of Southwest Africa. SWAPO, the guerrilla group
fighting for the independence of Southwest Africa (Namibia), also
endorsed the plan. Specifically, it included: (1) UN troops were
to supervise a ceasefire; (2) South African troops were to leave
Southwest Africa; (3) elections were to be held under UN
supervision; and (4) Walvis Bay, which had once been part of
Namibia under British colonial rule, was to be reunited with the
newly independent Namibia.

Members

Big Five was used to describe the states which were
considered most important at the end of World War II and which
possess special privileges in the United Nations. These states
were the United States, the United Kingdom, France, China, and the
Soviet Union. Until October, 1971, when the General Assembly
voted to give China's representation to the People's Republic of
China, that state was represented by delegates from Taiwan. The
Big Five special United Nations privileges consisted of: (1) a
permanent seat, together with veto power, in the Security Council;
(2) a permanent seat on the Trusteeship Council; and (3) repeated
election, through gentlemen's agreements, to the International
Court of Justice, the Economic and Social Council, and to the
Vice-Presidencies of the General Assembly. These latter positions

(Vice-Presidencies), in turn, provide automatic presence on the General Committee.

Because the permanent members of the Security Council are named in the Charter as "The Republic of China, France, the Union of Soviet Socialist Republics, the United Kingdom of Great Britain and Northern Ireland, the United States of America" (Article 23, Par. 1). A Charter amendment is necessary to alter the arrangement. Thus, over time, a discrepancy can occur between the power status of those members and the power reality within the international system, unless redressed by amendment.

In addition to their perpetual seat on the Council, permanent members possess the veto power over substantive questions and Charter amendments, with the qualification that a party to a dispute must abstain from voting in decisions under Chapter VI. Permanent members also hold automatic representation on the Military Staff Committee. Otherwise, permanent members have the same privileges as non-permanent members.

The nonpermanent members of the Security Council are elected for two-year terms (staggered) by the General Assembly (two-thirds majority required) with the Assembly presumably guided "in the first instance to the contribution of Members. . .to the maintenance of international peace and security and to the other purposes of the Organization, and also to equitable geographic distribution" (Article 23). In practice, seats are allocated primarily in terms of group-geographic factors (i.e., Latin American group) with little regard for the potential contribution of candidate states to the maintenance of peace and security. The number of non-permanent members was originally set at six, but has since been raised to ten through amendment of the Charter. Nonpermanent members are not elegible for immediate reelection. The major distinction, besides seat retention, between permanent and nonpermanent members lies in the veto power of the former.

The present (1980) non-permanent members of the Security Council are: Bangladesh, Bolivia, Czechoslovakia, Gabon, Jamaica, Kuwait, Nigeria, Norway, Portugal, and Zambia.

Organization and Procedures

The President of the Security Council is its principal officer, who exercises powers similar to those of the President of the General Assembly. Presidents of the Council are not elected; rather, each member of the Council holds the Presidency for one month, with the possession of the office rotating according to alphabetical order. The President of the Council may call meetings on his own initiative and also does so upon the request of a member of the Security Council or the Secretary-General or when a dispute is called to the attention of the Council by the General Assembly or a member state.

Each member of the Security Council, whether permanent or nonpermanent, has one vote. Nine or more affirmative votes decide procedural and substantive matters, with the qualification in respect to substantive matters that the resolution fails if a permanent member casts a negative vote, and that a party to a dispute shall not vote, when the Security Council operates under Chapter VI. These rules make the veto applicable to most Security Council decisions, except in the cases of election to the International Court of Justice, which requires a veto-free International Court of Justice, which requires a veto-free absolute majority decision, and agenda composition, decided by majority vote. These rules are a reflection of the supposed need to obtain agreement among the permanent ("great power") members on most important Security Council matters.

Although the term veto does not appear in the Charter, in usage it applies to the right of a permanent member of the Security Council to prevent a Security Council decision on substantive questions by a negative vote. The Charter provides, "Decisions of the Security Council on all other matters [other than procedural] shall be made by an affirmative vote of nine [previously seven] members including the concurring votes of the permanent members" (Article 27, Par. 3). This passage seems to imply that each of the permanent members must favor (cast a positive vote) in a decision or it is vetoed. In practice, however, neither physical absence from the Council, as that of the USSR at the beginning of the Korean War, or abstention have been viewed by the Council as constituting a veto. In the Korean example, on the other hand, the USSR did protest that her absence and other factors made the Security Council decisions, at that time, illegal. The use of the veto power is qualified by the provision that "in decisions under Chapter VI, and under paragraph 3 of Article 52, a party to a dispute shall abstain from voting" (Article 23, Par.3). Chapter VI refers to the use of resolutions to facilitate pacific settlement. Presumably then, each of the permanent members may lose its veto power if it is a party to a dispute and the Security Council is relying upon the above articles in its discussions. It is possible, however, for a permanent member to use its veto to prevent a Security Council determination that a conflict is a "dispute" and, therefore, retain its veto power in any attempted decisions on such matters. All of the permanent members have used their veto power. Veto power has been exercised by the USSR more than 100 times, by the United States fifteen times, by Great Britain ten times, by France four times, and by Communist China twice. While a member of the Security Council, Nationalist China used its veto twice.

The term, "double veto", is also used to describe certain procedures but does not appear in the Charter. It refers to the right of a permanent member to challenge the President of the Security Council in respect to his ruling as to whether a matter is procedural or substantive and then through the use of the veto make the matter substantive so that the veto applies in subsequent decisions.

Related to the use of the veto is the distinction between

procedural and substantive questions. A procedural question is one where the veto power of the permanent members of the Council does not normally apply. This includes such questions as the creation of subsidiary organs, the adoption of new rules of procedure, the bringing in of invited members, the place of meetings, and the passing of a question to the General Assembly. There is some ambiguity on these matters, however, in that, at times, questions that have been considered procedural have been made substantive through the exercise of the double veto. Agenda items themselves, however, are always considered procedural. General Assembly efforts to have the permanent members of the Security Council extend the list of questions considered procedural, to reduce the scope of the veto, have been unsuccessful.

A substantive question is one where the veto power of the permanent members of the Council may be exercised. This includes all important questions such as Charter amendments; a determination of a dispute or situation in respect to Chapter VI or Chapter VII; the application of sanctions; the recommendation of the appointment of the Secretary-General; and the admission, suspension, or expulsion of members.

Also important in the work of the Security Council is distinction between "situation" and dispute."

The term "situation" refers to an international development that can lead to "international friction," a "dispute," or "endanger the maintenance of international peace and security" (Charter, Article 34). The Security Council is authorized to investigate all such situations to determine whether the provisions of Chapter VI are applicable. If a determination concerning a situation does lead to the application of Chapter VI, a permanent member involved in the situation retains its veto power, in contrast to a dispute in which it is involved. If a situation is ascertained as likely to endanger the maintenance of international peace and security the Council may "recommend appropriate procedures or methods of adjustment" (Article 33, Par. 1). Any member of the United Nations can bring a situation to the attention of either the Security Council or the General Assembly.

A dispute refers to an international development where parties are in disagreement and which can possibly endanger the maintenance of international peace and security. The Security Council can investigate a dispute to see if it "is likely to endanger the maintenance of peace and security" (Article 34). If a dispute is deemed not likely to endanger peace and security, the Security Council may make recommendations with a view to pacific settlement methods (Article 33, Par. 2); recommend specific methods (Article 36, Par. 1); or, if (and only if) the parties bring the dispute to the Security Council after their failure to achieve a settlement by pacific means, "recommend such terms of settlement as it may consider appropriate" (Article 37, Par. 2).

Permanent members of the Security Council who are parties to a
dispute must abstain from voting when the Council is operating
under Chapter VI. A permanent member may use its veto, however,
to prevent the Council from considering a matter a dispute.
Disputes that actually threaten the peace are treated by the
Security Council under Chapter VII, where sanctions and use of
force are possible, but the veto always applies. Disputes may be
brought to the attention of the Security Council or General
Assembly by any member of the United Nations and by any nonmember
who is a party to a dispute that accepts "the obligations of
pacific settlement provided for in the present Charter" (Article
35, Par. 3).

Disarmament and Military Staff Committee Responsibilities

The Security Council, under Article 26, is charged with
"formulating, with the assistance of the Military Staff
Committee...plans to be submitted to the Members of the United
Nations for the establishment of a system for the regulation of
armaments." The guiding principle in respect to these plans is,
presumably, to maintain "international peace and security with the
least diversion for armaments of the world's human and economic
resources." Much of the Council's responsibility, in fact, has
been taken over historically by subsidiary organs such as the
Atomic Energy Commission, the Commission on Conventional
Armaments, and the Disarmament Commission. Also, a considerable
portion of disarmament negotiations has taken place between the
large nuclear powers outside of the United Nations. Thus, the
Security Council and the Military Staff Committee have never
really played the major role in disarmament envisioned by the
framers of the organization.

The history of Commission for Conventional Armaments
illustrates the ineffective efforts in this regard. It was
created by the Security Council, after a General Assembly
resolution of December, 1946, which stressed the international
need for the regulation and reduction of national armed forces.
The Commission's work was to focus on conventional armaments and,
therefore, to supplement but not overlap the work of the Atomic
Energy Commission (AEC). The Commission was composed of members
of the Security Council, both permanent and nonpermanent, and
reported to the Security Council. During Commission meetings,
disagreements between the Communist and other members centered on:
(1) the question of including weapons of mass destruction in the
Commission's work (Communists favored); (2) making the acceptance
of disarmament plans contingent upon the establishment of military
forces under the Security Council, the control of atomic energy,
and the conclusion of peace treaties with Japan and Germany
(Communists basically opposed preconditions); and (3) the nature
and function of international control and supervision (Communists
basically opposed extensive controls). Commission proposals, in

the form of a report approved by a Commission, noncommunist
majority, received a USSR veto in the Security Council in 1949.
Effective work by the Commission ended in April, 1950, when the
USSR withdrew, protesting the representation on the Commission of
the Republic of China instead of Communist China. The Commission
was disbanded in January, 1952, with the creation of the
Disarmament Commission.

The Military Staff Committee, composed of the Chiefs of Staff
of the permanent members of the Security Council or their
representatives, also indicates the futile nature of certain of
the Security Council efforts regarding controls on military forces
(in this case for enforcement purposes). The committee was to:
(1) advise the Security Council on force agreements and
requirements to maintain peace and security; (2) give strategic
direction, under the Security Council, for armed forces at the
disposal of the Security Council; and (3) advise and assist the
Security Council in respect to the regulation of armaments
(Article 26, Par. 47). The Military Staff Committee first met in
February, 1946, and shortly thereafter considered, upon the
Security Council's request, the problem of bringing forces under
the Security Council as provided for in Article 43. The
Committee's report of April, 1947, revealed disagreements between
the major powers, especially between the US and the USSR,
particularly on the questions of: (1) the size of the forces; (2)
the location of the forces when not used by the Security Council;
(3) the balance of the forces; and (4) arrangements concerning use
of bases and facilities. In general, the USSR wanted smaller,
balanced forces (each member to contribute the same force
components) stationed, when not in use, in the donating country;
the United States preferred larger forces (composed of what each
member was best able to contribute) stationed to the best
advantage of the Security Council, even when not in use. Although
agreement was reached upon a number of other points (twenty-five
in all) the above contentious points and certain others led the
Committee to report, in July, 1948, that further progress was not
possible. Since then, the Committee has been basically
nonfunctional, with its armament regulation functions absorbed by
various commissions and its strategic direction functions provided
on an ad hoc basis when United Nations forces are employed, as in
the Korean crisis.

Special Historic Groups and Forces of the Security Council

Historically important groups and forces relating to the
efforts of the Security Council in various crises include: the
United Nations Observation Group, Operation of the United Nations
in the Congo, United Nations Observation Mission in Yemen, United
Nations Peace Keeping Force in Cyprus, United Nations Emergency
Force, United Nations Emergency Force II, United Nations
Disengagement Observer Force, the United Nations Commission for

the Unification and Rehabilitation of Korea, and the United
Nations Interim Force in Lebanon.

United Nations Observation Group

The United Nations Observation Group was formed by the
Security Council in 1958, during the Lebanon crisis, for the
purposes of observing the Lebanese borders to detect the passage
of illegal personnel or arms into Lebanon. The Secretary-General
was authorized to compose the force and did so out of the United
Nations Truce Supervisory Organization located in Jerusalem. The
peak strength of the group amounted to approximately 600 persons.
The mission lasted from June-December 1958, during which time
conditions sufficiently improved to terminate it.

Operation of the United Nations in the Congo

The United Nations Force for the Congo was formed following a
request of Secretary-General Hammarskjold to the Security Council
in July 13, 1960. The chronic situation in the Republic of the
Congo was brought to the attention of the Secretary-General after
Congolese independence was granted on June 30, 1960. The Security
Council supported the Secretary-General's request on JUly 14, and
gave him a mandate to compose a force to support the Congolese
government. The Security Council resolution also requested that
Belgium remove her troops from the Congo. Within a few days,
Secretary-General Hammarskjold dispatched the initial contingent
of approximately 3500 men. Moise Tshombe, President of Katanga,
however, refused to allow the entry of ONUC into Katanga Province
and, although Belgium removed her troops from the other portions
of the Congo, they remained in Katanga. On August 8, the Security
Council authorized the Secretary-General to have ONUC enter
Katanga in order to implement the original resolution. The
purpose of the mission was to take up areas of control vacated by
Belgium troops. The Soviet Union, however, called for the
complete suppression of Tshombe by United Nations forces and this
demand was also made by Patrice Lumumba, the Premier of the
Central Government. Disputes over this matter, and others, led to
a deadlock in the Security Council. On the iniative of the United
States, the Uniting for Peace Resolution was used to bring the
matter into the General Assembly in September. In the meantime,
the governmental situation in the Congo had become fragmented and
disorganized. The General Assembly, in spite of USSR disapproval,
supported the Secretary-General's policies in respect to the Congo
and his decisions concerning the application of force. When
competing delegations from the Congo arrived, to be seated in the
General Assembly, one headed by Congo President Kasavubu and the
other by Lumumba, the Kasavubu delegation was seated. This
further alienated the Soviet Union and certain other states from
the Congo operation. Charges by the Soviet Union were further

intensified after the assassination of Lumumba on February, 1961. On February 21, 1961, the Security Council again considered the matter and authorized the Secretary-General to take any measures necessary to prevent a civil war in the Congo and called for the withdrawal of Belgium and other foreign military troops. ONUC gradually grew to 23,000 men and intensive fighting developed between ONUC and the Katanga forces. After negotiations between the two sides, a cease fire was arranged on September 21, 1961, and it was agreed that foreign troops were to be removed from Katanga. The Security Council further strengthened the Secretary-General's hand on November 13, when it authorized him to use forceful means if necessary to remove foreign military troops and the Council declared its support for the Congo Central Government. Fighting resumed, however, between ONUC and Katanga forces. Finally, in December, Tshombe decided, in view of defeats, to promise cooperation in the formation of a new government. Sporadic fighting continued, however, until January, 1963, after which Tshombe sought asylum in Spain. After completing pacification, ONUC forces were gradually reduced until June 30, 1964, when they were withdrawn. Although ONUC was successful in its general mission of preventing fragmentation of the Congo, the operation was a costly one. The United Nations became deeply involved in a situation which alienated a number of states and which accentuated the financial crisis connected with peace-keeping operations.

United Nations Observation Mission in Yemen

The United Nations Observation Mission in Yemen was created by the Security Council in 1963 to observe and to report on the situation in Yemen in view of possible armed conflict between the United Arab Republic and Saudi Arabia. These states have actively supported opposite sides since the overthrow of the Yemen monarchy. After protracted conflict, a settlement between the parties was reached in August, 1965. In spite of this, however, tension and hostilities continued and Yemen suffered a civil war which split the Arab nation.

United Nations Peace Keeping Force in Cyprus

In February, 1964, the Security Council recommended that the General Assembly constitute a peace-keeping force for Cyprus (UNFICYP), in view of fighting between Greek and Turkish Cypriots and the possibility of an armed clash between Greece and Turkey over the matter. The basic purpose of the force (UNFICYP) was to pacify the situation by standing between the fighting groups. The force was expanded to approximately 6000 by June, 1964. Since then, the United Nations has attempted numerous techniques to attempt to bring the two sides together and has repeatedly extended the life of UNIFCYP beyond its initial three-months duration. Each six-month extension has been granted with the pronounced hope that by its expiration sufficient progress will have been made to allow drastic reduction in, or total disbanding of, the Force. Remarkably enough, UNFICYP, which depends on voluntary financing, has not sustained a budget deficit; even though it has cost $286.1 million. During the Turkish invasion of Cyprus in July, 1974, UNFICYP consisted of 2,300 troops, to which 1,400 were added on July 30 (British, Danish, Finnish and Swedish additions). Services of the UN High Commissioner for Refugees were enlisted for the 226,000 homeless Cypriots. Forty members of UNFICYP were killed in Cyprus during 1974. Turkey justified the invasion in order to "protect the Turkish community there" and occupied Kyrenia to Nicosia. By August 16, 1974, Turkey had occupied the northern one-third of the island. Although Turkey submitted a plan for a federal system in Cyprus, Greece refused to negotiate after the Turkish occupation and ceasefire in August-December, 1974. The situation was still stalemated at the beginning of 1980.

United Nations Emergency Force II

In 1967, Abdul Gamal Nassar, President of Egypt, ordered the United Nations Emergency Force (established by the General Assembly) to leave the Sinai buffer zone. Israel then launched a pre-emptive strike against Egypt, thus beginning the Six-Day War. In October,1973, Egypt's new president, Sadat, launched a surprise attack against Israeli forces on the Suez canal. After fierce fighting, a cease-fire was called and UNEF II was sent in to stand between the two forces. UNEF II was renewed by the Security Council for a one year period on October 21, 1977 and for a nine month period on October 23, 1978 and was terminated in 1979.

United Nations Disengagement Observer Force

UNDOF was sent as a result of the six day Yom Kipper war between Israel and Syria. The initial task was to take over territory evacuated in stages by Israel, in accordance with a disengagement aggreement to establish a zone of separation. The Force continues to man the zone and Syrian and Israli forces are excluded. It also carries out inspections in areas of limited armaments and forces and attempts to preserve the cease-fire. The zone of separation is presently under civilian administration.

United Nations Commission for thr Unification and Rehabilitation of Korea

The UN Commission for the Unification and Rehabilitation of Korea (UNCURK) originated in the aftermath of the Korean War. The UN had maintained a military command in South Korea since its inception in 1950 when it served the purpose of helping to repel

the North Korean attack against South Korea. By 1975 the UN force
had reduced to about 100 troops, mostly Americans. The US,
however, seperately maintained 40,000 troops in South Korea. The
US submitted a plan to end the UN Command in South Korea on
January 1, 1976 provided that China and North Korea agreed to an
alternative mechanism of implementing the 1953 armistice accord.
(US troops in South Korea were authorized by separate 1974 accord
between the US-South Korea; thus, they would remain unaffected by
the offer.) The plan was adopted and UNCORK ended in 1978.

United Nations Interim Force in Lebanon

The UN Interim Force in Lebanon (UNIFIL) was created to ensure
that war-torn country's peaceful transition to stability. The
functions of UNIFIL, begun in March,1978, are to confirm the
withdrawal of Israeli forces, to restore inte ᴧational peace and
security, and to assist the Government of Lebanon in ensuring the
return of its effective authority in southern Lebanon. Its force
is a composite of Polish, Irish, Finnish, Syrian, French, and
Senegalese troops. Its existence, unless extended, ends May
31,1981.

United Nations Truce Supervision Organization Jerusalem

UNTSO was established initially to supervise the truce called
by the Security Council in May 1948 in the war between Egypt and
Israel. Basically it assisted in the application of the 1949
Armistice Agreement. Presently it's observers assist other
peacekeeping forces in the area as an integral part of their
operations.

THE ECONOMIC AND SOCIAL COUNCIL

The Economic and Social Council is designated as a principal
organ of the United Nations (Article 7) and is responsible for
promoting the objectives, set forth in Chapter IX of the Charter,
concerning international economic and social cooperation. This
includes concern with the promotion of "higher standards of
living, full employment, and conditions of economic and social
progress and development; solutions of international economic,
social, health, and related problems; international cultural and
educational cooperation; and universal respect for and observance
of human rights and fundamental freedoms for all without distinction as to race, sex, language, or religion." In connection with
these responsibilities, the Economic and Social Council
may make and initiate studies and make recommendations
to the General Assembly, member states, or the specialized agencies. Within its sphere of competence, the
Council may draft international conventions for submission to the General Assembly, call for international
conferences, and perform special services at the request
of member states.
Specialized agencies which also operate in the economic,
social, cultural, educational, health, and related fields are
coordinated by the Economic and Social Council in terms of
agreements reached between these agencies and the Council.
In all of its work, the Council operates "under the authority
of the General Assembly." Thus, such matters as the nature of
agreements with the specialized agencies, the calling of
international conferences and the submission of draft resolutions
to member states must win the approval of the General Assembly.
In fact, two of the General Assembly's main committees -- the
Economic and Financial and the Social, Humanitarian, and Cultural
-- devote a considerable portion of their attention to the
Economic and Social Council's work.
The Council, because of its variegated objectives and the
wide-flung nature of the numerous organs reporting to it and
working with it, has been constantly plagued with the problem of
coordination and integration of the activities for which it is
responsible.

Members

Members of the Economic and Social Council are elected by the
General Assembly (two-thirds majority) for three-year staggered
terms with eligibility for reelection (Article 61). Prior to an
amendment to the Charter, effective for the actual membership on
January 1, 1973, the Council had 27 members. Since then, the
membership has been 54. The Council may invite members of the UN

and arrange for representatives of specialized agencies to participate without vote in Council deliberations. (Articles 69, 70). The "Big Five" with the exception of China have always been elected by the Assembly to the Council, although the UN Charter does not require it.

Sessions

The Council normally holds both spring and summer sessions of approximately four to six weeks each year. The second session is reconvened after the General Assembly's session to consider the Assembly's resolution relative to the Council's work and to plan for new sessions. Special sessions are held upon the call of the Security Council, General Assembly, or a majority of the members of the Council. Members of the United Nations and specialized agencies may request special sessions which will be held if the President and Vice-Presidents of the Council agree or a majority of Council members concur. Also, the President may call meetings if the Vice-Presidents agree.

Voting

Each member of the Economic and Social Council has one vote and decisions are made by a simple majority of those present and voting (Article 67). Although the permanent members of the Security Council have always been elected to the Council, they possess no special privileges.

The Economic and Social Council may, if it is deemed desirable, because the matter under discussion is of particular concern to a member of the United Nations, invite that member without a vote to participate in the Council discussions (Charter, Article 69).

Relations with Nongovernmental Organizations

Nongovernmental Organizations (NGO's) are private groups, such as the International Chamber of Commerce or the World Federation of Trade Unions, which, according to Article 71 of the Charter, may enter into consultation with the Economic and Social Council, through arrangements of consultative status. In this connection, they are classified as "category A", "category B", or"category R".

"Category A" refers to non-governmental organizations (NGO's) which have been given this status because of the high degree of relationship between their work and that of the Council. Organizations so classified are the International Chamber of Commerce, International Confedration of Free Trade Unions, International Co-operative Alliance, International Federation of Agricultural Producers. International Federation of Christian Trade Unions, International Organization of Employees, Inter-Parliamentary Union, World Federation of Trade Unions, World

Federation of United Nations Associations, and World Veterans
Federation. The "rights" of these organizations are greater than
those in "category B." They include the right to: (1) propose
items for the provisional agenda of the Council and its
commissions (may not be accepted), (2) submit written statements
(2000 words or less) to the Council and its commissions, (3)
observe public meetings, (4) consult with standing committees of
the Council upon request, and (5) appear before the Council upon
recommendation of a standing committee. Organizations are
reviewed annually in respect to their status.

"Category B" refers to non-governmental organizations (NGO's)
given this status because they have interest in certain aspects of
the Council's work. Approximately 120 organizations, including
various business, professional, economic, social, and religious
groups, hold the "B" rating and they possess fewer "rights" than
those organizations in "Category A." Category B organizations
have the right to: (1) submit written statements to the Council
(500 words) and commissions (2000 words), (2) observe public
meetings, and (3) consult with Council committees upon request.
NGO's are reviewed annually in respect to their status.

Category R is applicable to those organizations which "can
make occasional and useful contributions to the work of the
Council."

Committee on Nongovernmental Organizations

The Committee on Nongovernmental Organizations, consisting of
seven members elected by the Council from Council members each
year with the Council's President serving ex officio, screens
nongovernmental organizations requesting consultative status and
makes recommendations to the Council concerning their status. It
also considers, with the power of rejection, provisional agenda
items proposed by organizations in Category A.

Regional Economic Commissions

The Economic and Social Council, as authorized by Article 68
of the UN Charter, has established five regional economic
commissions -- the Economic Commission for Africa (ECA), the
Economic Commission for Asia and the Pacific (ESCAP), the Economic
Commission for Europe (ECE), the Economic Commission for Latin
America (ECLA), and the Economic Commission for West Asia (ECWA).
The commissions include the members of the United Nations located
in the region concerned and, possibly, certain non-United Nations
members in the region, as well as non-regional members who have a
special concern in the region. The commissions strive for regional, economic development through data collection and exchange
of information and also initiate and coordinate projects.
Commission functions are facilitated through the creation of
various committees, subcommittees, and subsidiary organs. Each

full commission meets regularly, reports to the Economic and Social Council, has a budget (which is part of the United Nations
regular budget) and a permanent Secretariat. Valuable economic
survey data and economic bulletins are published by the
commission.

The Economic Commission for Africa was created, on April 29,
1958, as a regional, economic commission under the Council. The
Commission originally included all of the United Nations members
of Africa (as well as France, Spain, Portugal, and the United
Kingdom as especially interested states). Since 1963, however,
South Africa has been suspended and Portugal was excluded from the
Commission. The headquarters and Secretariat are located in Addis
Ababa, Ethiopia, where the annual sessions are held. The
headquarters provide a centralized location for the fifty members
and for 450 staff. The Commission gathers information on and
fosters state cooperation in respect to matters such as
agriculture, population growth, trade conservation, transport,
power, resources, money, and education. For example, ECA helped
organize and sponsor the Conference of African States on the
Development of Education (1961). The Commission reports to the
Council and publishes the Economic Bulletin for Africa. In 1976,
the ECA published its Revised Framework of Principles for the
Implementation of the New International Economic Order in Africa,
1976-1981-1986.

The present budget is set at approximately $19,000,000.

Magee in his "ECA and Paradox of African Cooperation" examines
the ECA and finds that its African member states care very little
about the organization as an integrative institution.

The Economic Commission for Asia and the Pacific was created,
on March 28, 1947, as a regional, economic commission under the
Council. The Commission includes all of the United Nations
members in the Asian and Far Eastern area (Iran eastward). Also
included are France, Netherlands, USSR, United Kingdom, and the
United States as non-Asian interested states, and South Korea as a
non-United Nation Asian state. Papua New Guinea participated for
the first time in 1972. The headquarters and Secretariat are
located in Bangkok, Thailand; although, the place of the annual
sessions rotates among the regional member states. Through
committees and bureaus, the Commission acquires information on and
facilitates state cooperation in respect to transportation,
communications, industrialization, exploitation of minerals,
trade, flood control, and related matters in the Asian and Far
Eastern area. In 1966, the Commission launched the Asian
Development Bank, whose resources would be open to members of the
UN or its specialized agencies, as well as those in the ESCAP
geographical region. The Commission reports to the Council and
publishes The Economic Survey of Asia and the Far east (Annual),
The Economic Bulletin of Asia and the Far East (Quarterly), and
more specialized materials such as the Mineral Resources Development series. ESCAP's 1978/79 budget was $19,404,800.

The Economic Commission for Europe was created, on March 28, 1947, as a regional, economic commission under the Council. All United Nations members in the European area are members of the Commission, including the USSR, Byelorussia, Ukraine, the United Kingdom and the United States as a non-European interested state. Switzerland holds a consultative status in respect to the Commission and its subsidiary organs. Those invited to participate on a consultative basis are not allowed to vote. The headquarters and permanent Secretariat are located in Geneva, where the annual meetings are held. Much of the work of the Commission is facilitated by committees that focus upon particular problems, such as agriculture, electrical power, transportation, housing, trade, timber and steel, and examine such problems as supply, demand, qualtiy cycles, trends and stablization. Neither the Commission nor its committees possesses any decision making power, but their recommendations may lead to treaties. The Commission reports to the Council and publishes The Economic Survey of Europe (Annual) and Economic Bulletin for Europe (Quarterly) as well as specialized bulletins dealing with electrical,housing, and agricultural statistics.

Myrdal, in "Twenty Years of the United Nations Economic Commission for Europe" assesses the Commission's record (where he had been executive secretary from 1947-1957) and concludes that the ECE has been able to employ the improved political climate to work successfully. Nevertheless, Myrdal suggested the machinery of the Commission needs strengthening.

The 1978-79 budget was set at $19,014,200.

The Economic Commission for Latin America was created on February 25, 1948, as a regional, economic commission under the Council. The Commission includes all of the United Nations members in the Latin American area and Canada, France, Netherlands, United Kingdom and the United States as especially interested states. The headquarters and Secretariat are located in Santiago, Chile; although, the place of Commission sessions rotates among member states. The Commission, through various subgroups, makes studies and facilitates cooperation in respect to matters such as population, growth, trade, industry, labor, government efficiency, and economic integration. ECLA, for example, was actively involved in the creation of the Latin American Free Trade Area. The Commission reports to the Council and is responsible for THE Economic Survey of Latin America (Annual), the Economic Bulletin for Latin America (semi-annual), and other technical publications.

The 1977-78 budget was set at approximately $20,000,000.

The Economic Commission for West Asia was created on August 9, 1973 as a regional, economic commission under the Council. The Commission includes 12 members: Bahrain, Democratic Yemen, Egypt, Iraq, Jordan, Kuwait, Lebanon, Oman, Palestine Liberation Organization, Qatar, Saudi Arabia, Syrian Arab Republic, United Arab Emirates, and Yemen. Israel is not a member of the

organization, and there are no non-regional members. Headquarters
are located at Beirut.
The Commission was designed to promote the economic
reconstruction and development of West Asia. At the May, 1976
meeting in Doha, Qatar it was resolved to study the economic and
social situation of the region, as well as the potential of the
Palestinian Arabs. At the fourth session during April 24-29, 1977
in Amman, Jordan ECWA voted to increase aid to rebuild Lebanon and
approved its work program for 1978-1979. The latter favored the
less-developed members. Egypt and the PLO were also considered
with reference to their becoming full Commission members. Other
resolutions concerned regional development and oil as a
transnational industry. ECWA publishes documents related to the
economic and social aspects of the area.
The 1977-78 budget was set at $10,566,000.

Functional Commissions

Functional Commissions are created to aid the Council and are
authorized by Article 68 of the Charter. They focus on particular
problems without geographic boundaries, in contrast to the
Regional Economic Commissions. With the exception of the
Commission on Narcotic Drugs (composed of important drug
manufacturing states and ones with serious illegal drug traffic)
the member states of the Commissions are elected by the Council to
achieve geographic balance. Some Commissions, such as
Statistical, International Commodity, and Population, focus upon
technical data acquisition and analysis. Others, such as the
Social Commission, Commission on Human Rights, and Commission on
the Status of Women, combine data collection functions with
recommendations as to policy. The Narcotics Commission, in
addition to these functions, possesses a limited supervisory power
based on conventions. The Commissions operate in a manner similar
to the Council with a chairman, vice-chairman, and majority vote
rule. Some meet annually and others every two years. Much
important data published by the United Nations is the result of
the work of the Commissions.
The work of the functional commissions is illustrated by the
Commission on Narcotic Drugs, consisting of representatives
appointed by the Council from twenty-four states which are
important drug producers or which have a serious problem with
illicit drug traffic. The Commission: (1) advises the Council on
conventions relating to drug control; (2) investigates and advises
on United Nations-related drug control machinery; (3) reviews and
advises on individual countries' control measures; (4)
investigates new drugs as to their danger and use and makes
recommendations; and (5) can invite other organs, such as the
World Health Organization, to undertake studies. The Commission
reports to the Council and its recommendations may form the basis
of Council and/or General Assembly recommendations. In general,

the Commission forms the central organ of the drug control system
and carries on the work of the League of Nations' Advisory
Committee on Traffic in Opium and Other Dangerous Drugs. In
recent years, the Commission has increased its activities. The
report of its twenty-fourth session (1971) reflected this
expansion by generating the 1971 convention on Psychotropic
Substances. In this connection, a Sub-Commission for Illicit Drug
Traffic and Related Matters in the Near and Middle East has been
created to monitor and deal with illegal traffic in the area.

Special Bodies

     "Special bodies" refers to certain Council-related organs
that do not fit into the category of specialized agencies,
functional commissions, or regional economic commissions, such as
the United Nations Children's Fund (treated under the General
Assembly) and the International Narcotics Control Board in New
York.
     Two drug agencies preceeded the creation of the International
Narcotics Control Board; the Permanent Central Opium Board and the
Drug Supervisory Body.
     The Permanent Central Opium Board was created by the
International Opium Convention of 1925. Its purpose and functions
under the League of Nations continued under the United Nations.
Eight independent experts were appointed, as such, for five-year
terms by the Council to form the Board which had the primary duty
of scrutinizing the reports of states required under the
Convention as to the production, consumption, import, and export
of narcotic drugs. State violations of drug conventions could
have led, under the Convention, to consultation, inquiry (with
permission), embargo on drugs, and, of course, publicity by the
Board. The Board met twice a year and reported to the Council.
After the Single Convention on Narcotic Drugs came into force on
December 13, 1964, the functions of the Central Opium Board were
combined with those of the Drug Supervisory Commission to form the
new single agency.
     The Drug Supervisory Body was created in 1931 by the
Convention for Limiting the Manufacturing and Regulating the
Distribution of Drugs. Its functions under the League System
continued under the United Nations. Four independent experts, two
apppointed by the World Health Organization, one by the Permanent
Central Opium Board, and one by the Commission of Narcotic Drugs,
reviewed drug needs estimated by states and had the power to
request revisions and explanations of estimates. States were
limited in respect to their import and manufacture of drugs to
limits based upon their estimates. The Supervisory Body reported
to the Council and issued a publication entitled ESTIMATED WORLD
REQUIREMENTS OF NARCOTIC DRUGS. The single Convention on Narcotic
Drugs was the instrument by which the two bodies were combined.
It was adopted by a special conference held for that purpose at

the United Nations in January—March, 1961. As of June, 1972, a
total of eighty-five states were parties to the Convention. The
Single Convention coalesces previous treaties in the narcotics
area and establishes a tighter system of control. An
eleven-member International Narcotics Control Board, increased to
thirteen members in 1972, is responsible for the overall
coordination and supervision of the drug abuse control treaties as
they are implemented by member states. As noted, the Board
absorbed the powers and functions of the Central Opium Board and
the Drug Supervisory Body. The Board meets twice a year in order
to survey the world drug situation. The Secretariat of the
International Narcotics Control Board has processed information
from 170 governments. The headquarters in Geneva were scheduled
to move to Donaupark, Vienna in 1979.

Technical Assistance and Disaster Relief

Significant Economic and Social Council economic assistance
began with the Expanded Program of Technical Assistance which grew
out of an Ecomonic and Social Council request, in February, 1949,
to the effect that the Secretary-General and heads of the
specialized agencies formulate a comprehensive plan to provide
technical assistance to underdeveloped areas. Upon the Council's
acceptance of the plan, recommendations to establish a program
were made to the General Assembly and the Program became
operational in July, 1950. Prior to this, although the United
Nations had engaged in various types of assistance, it had been on
a very limited scale. The new Program established a basis for aid
in respect to technical assistance, fellowships, training grants,
and certain types of material assistance. These activities are
qualified, however, by the provisions that a recipient state
request aid; decide upon the kind of aid to be given; and
cooperate with administering agencies, in respect to such matters
as information and publicity. Also, assistance could not be used
to interfere in the internal affairs of recipients.
The Program was carried out by a Technical Assistance Board
and Technical Assistance Committee.
Various agencies participated in the program, such as UNESCO,
Food and Agricultural Organization, International Labor
Organization, International Civil Aviation Organization,
Inter-Governmental Maritime Consultative Organization, World
Health Organization, World Meteorological Organization,
International Telecommunications Union, Universal Postal Union,
International Atomic Energy Agency, and the Secretariat of the
United Nations. Funds were contributed by both United Nations
members and other states on a voluntary basis, through pledging
conferences, and were allocated by the General Assembly after
recommendations of the Economic and Social Council, Technical
Assistance Committee, and Technical Assistance Board.
The Technical Assistance Committee was a major organ in the

Expanded Program of Technical Assistance. It was composed of
thirty representatives, eighteen of which come from ECOSOC member
states. The rest were elected by ECOSOC. It reported to ECOSOC
on the coordination, effectiveness, and activities of the Expanded
Program and authorized the allocation of funds to participating
agencies.

The Technical Assistance Board, created in 1950, consisted of
an executive chairman, appointed by the Secretary-General, and
heads of all specialized agencies participating in the United
Nations Expanded Program of Technical Assistance. This included
agencies such as the International Labor Organization, World
Health Organization, World Meteorological Organization, and the
United Nations Educational, Scientific, and Cultural Organization.
TAB maintained offices and representatives in the many countries
receiving United Nations aid, which assisted receiving governments
in drawing up developmental plans and helped coordinate the work
of the various agencies giving aid. National requests for aid
were consolidated and related to existing funds by TAB which then
submitted a general aid program to the Technical Assistance
Committee. Also important was the Special Fund. The Special Fund
was created on January 1, 1959, by a resolution of the General
Assembly. Its purpose was to stimulate the economic development
of less developed countries by facilitating investments in
important projects. The Fund operated preinvestment areas in
partnership with recipient governments. Primarily, then, it
stimulated further investment by investing in survey training,
education, and research projects. Much was accomplished in
cooperation with and through other international agencies, such as
the International Labor Organization and the Food and Agricultural
Organization. Projects were financed through voluntary
contributions raised through pledging conferences. Structurally,
the Fund was administered by a Managing Director who made
recommendations in respect to projects reviewed by consultative
boards and approved by an eighteen-member Governing Council. The
Council was divided between economically advanced and economically
developing states.

In August, 1964, in the interest of coordination, the
Economic and Social Council recommended that the Expanded Program
be consolidated with the Special Fund in a new program entitled
the United Nations Development Program (effective January 1 1966).
Distinctions between the Special Fund and the Expanded Program of
Technical Assistance were eliminated as of January, 1972, when the
merger of the two components of the United Nations Development
Program was completed and the primary organ of coordination became
the Governing Council. The Governing Council consists of
representatives of 48 countries, both industrial and developing.
It is the policy-making body of the UNDP. One-third of its
membership changes yearly. (For further information on the UNDP
see Special Declarations, Programs, Resolutions and Conferences.)

Before its merger with the Special Fund, the Expanded Program

had provided technical assistance amounting to over $540,000,000.
A Disaster Relief Office headed by the Disaster Relief
Coordinator was created by a resolution passed by the General
Assembly on December 14, 1971. The office was established at
Geneva. In addition to coordinating disaster relief, the
Coordinator was charged to promote the study, prevention, control,
and prediction of natural disasters; to receive contributions and
disseminate those which are earmarked for disaster relief; to
advise governments on predisaster planning; and to prepare an
annual report for the Secretary-General. Initial authorizations
were for $200,000, with no more than $20,000 going to any one
country for a single disaster. All members of the United Nations
were invited to join the Disaster Relief Office, as well as all
other interested organizations.

Specialized and Other Agencies

The Economic and Social Council helps coordinate the following
United Nations specialized agencies, most of which have a high
degree of autonomy: UNICEF, UNHCR, UNDP, UN/FAO, and the
International Narcotics Control Board.

The Food and Agricultural Organization

The Food and Agricultural Organization came into existence on
October 16, 1945, after approval of its constitution by more than
twenty states. The constitution was drawn up by an interim
commission formed at the United Nations Conference on Food and
Agriculture held at Hot Springs, Virginia, in May-June of 1943.
FAO became a specialized agency of the Unted Nations in December,
1946, reporting to the Economic and Social Council. The major
purposes of the organization are to foster food and agricultural
production, efficiency, consumption, and distribution; to further
the living conditions of "rural populations"; and to contribute,
generally, toward expanding the world's economy. In this
capacity, FAO collects, analyzes, interprets, and disseminates
information and makes recommendations regarding research,
education, administration, conservation, processing, marketing,
distribution, credit, and commodity arrangements. In addition, it
furnishes a wide range of technical assistance including the
dispatch of aid missions to assist states in resolving various
problems related to the organization's primary functions. FAO has
been active in fostering interstate cooperation for the prevention
of starvation and has been involved in various projects such as
the restoration of land fertility, river basin development,
improvement of seeds and fertilizers, and development of
preventive measures against numerous diseases connected with
agricultural production. FAO coordinates the Freedom-from-Hunger
Campaign, and, in collaboration with the United Nations,
administers the World Food Program. Problems connected with

forest production and conservation have also been dealt with as well as efforts toward drought assistance.

The primary organs to accomplish these objectives are the Conference, the Council, and the Director-General (Secretariat).

The Conference, which meets in Rome in odd-numbered years, is composed of representatives from member states and is the major policy-making body of FAO. It may make recommendations on the numerous matters related to the organization's functions either to individual states, to the Council, or to other international organizations. Conventions on FAO matters and amendments to the FAO Constitution must be approved by the Conference prior to submission to member states. The Conference elects the members of the Council, the Director-General, and adopts the FAO budget. Each member state exercises one vote in the Conference.

The Council consists of forty-nine member states elected by the Conference for two-year terms and acts on behalf of the Conference between its sessions. In this capacity, the Council supervises the Secretariat, the regional offices, and the regional and functional bodies. It also makes estimates as to the basic food and agricultural situation and has the right to make recommendations to member states and to international agencies in respect to such matters. The Council members always reflect a wide geographic balance.

The Director-General, elected by the Conference, operates under the policy guidelines set down by the Conference and the Council and directs the Secretariat, consistng of approximately 5000 persons, including more than 4,088 experts working on projects in the field. Secretariat members are distributed between the permanent headquarters in Rome and the various regional and subregional offices in the world's major, geographic subdivisions. The Secretariat services the other organs of FAO and is involved in numerous technical and assistance functions.

Membership is open through a simple ratification for those states named in the FAO Constitution, forty-five in all, who served on the Interim Commission producing the constitution. Other states are admitted, upon application, through a two-thirds absolute majority vote of approval by the members of the Conference. The Soviet Union, which served on the Interim Commission, has not chosen to accept membership. South Africa terminated its membership in December of 1964. Presently there are 144 full members.

Once a two-year budget is decided upon by the Conference, member states are assessed according to a scale of contributions based on ability to pay. For example, the United States is responsible for approximately 30% of the budget while the United Kingdom has responsibility for 10%. The 1978/79 budget amounted to $211.3 million. In addition, FAO spends several million dollars as a participant in the United Nations Development Program.

Many of the members of FAO have formed national committees

composed of various officials and representatives of organizations having a bearing on FAO's work. These committees maintain a liaison with the Secretariat and advise their home governments in respect to FAO policies. In addition, they may promote FAO objectives and understanding through publications, meetings, and lectures.

The World Food Program, initiated by the Food and Agricultural Organization and the United Nations in 1961, with a $100 million basic pledge, consists of an effort to utilize voluntary contributions of money, services, and food to counteract local food emergency stiuations; to create national food reserves; to facilitate school and pre-school nutrition; and to aid in food development projects. A twenty-four nation committee, twelve of whose members are elected by FAO and twelve by the Economic and Social Council of the United Nations, directs the program. It has been used frequently in emergency aid situations. For instance, food was provided for victims of the tidal wave which struck East Pakistan in 1970, for the Palestinian refugees in the Near East, and for twenty-eight emergency operations in twenty-three countries in the year 1971. The Program has been aided by FAO, ILO, WHO, and UNESCO, as well as by the United Nations Development Program. In 1977, the Food Security Assistance Scheme helped thirteen countries to ensure adequate food supplies.

FAO publishes numerous materials dealing with projections, trends, and surveys, as well as yearbooks, such as The Yearbook of Fishery Statistics.

THE INTER-GOVERMENTAL MARITIME CONSULTATIVE ORGANIZATION

The convention for IMCO was drafted by the United Nations Maritime Conference sponsored by the United Nations Economic and Social Council held in February-March, 1948. The convention came into effect in March, 1958, when 21 states ratified it. IMCO became a specialized agency of the United Nations in January, 1959, following an agreement between the General Assembly and the IMCO Assembly.

The basic purposes of the organization are to promote interstate cooperation on standards of sea safety and technical matters concerning maritime trade and to discourage restrictive and discriminatory trade practices. IMCO has become increasingly involved in international water pollution control matters. In 1969, 1971, and 1973 IMCO convened international conferences on oil pollution out of which have come the Convention for the Prevention of the Pollution of the Sea by Oil, the International Convention Relating to Intervention on the High Seas in Cases of Oil Pollution Casualties, and the International Convention on Civil Liability for Oil Pollution Damage. All of these were ratified in 1975. Also, IMCO has established an International Fund for Compensation for Oil Pollution Damage by Ships. Generally, IMCO makes recommendations to states and interstate

agencies; drafts conventions; oversees certain maritime
conventions already in effect; sponsors conferences; engages in
technical studies, such as those concerning signal codes and
tonnage measurements; and disseminates information.

Original United Nations Maritime Conference members and
members of the United Nations may become members of IMCO by
accepting its convention. Other states may become members by
accepting the convention if they receive the approval of
two-thirds of the IMCO membership. West Germany and Switzerland,
for example, have been admitted under these procedures.
Territories not responsible for their international relations may
become associate members if the responsible state is already a
member. By 1980, there were 107 members in the organization. The
USSR and the Eastern European Communist states, with the exception
of Albania, belonged to IMCO. As in the case of other specialized
agencies, the Communist states of Vietnam and North Korea are not
members.

The principal organs of IMCO are the Assembly, the Council,
the Maritime Safety Committee, and the Secretary-General
(Secretariat). The headquarters are located in London.

The Assembly consists of representatives from all the member
states and is the basic policy-making organ of IMCO. Besides
establishing the basic work program of the organization, it
approves the budget, establishes financial and staff regulations,
elects the Council, and approves appointment of the
Secretary-General by the Council. The Assembly meets in regular
session every two years. The Assembly can also convene
conferences, as for instance, its decision to convene an
International Conference on Marine Pollution in 1973.

The Council, consists of twenty-four member states. It
carries on the work of the organization between sessions of the
Assembly and normally meets twice a year. Council members are
elected by the Assembly according to the following guidelines:
six Council seats go to states with the largest interest in
seaborne trade; six seats go to states with the largest interest
in shipping services; and twelve seats go to states with special
interests in maritime transport or navigation and whose election
will give geographic balance to the Council. Besides supervising
the basic work program and the Secretariat, the Council appoints
the Secretary-General and drafts recommendations and conventions
subject to the approval of the Assembly.

The Maritime Safety Committee is formed by one representative
from each member state. The primary function of the Committee is
to consider problems of maritime safety and to make
recommendations to the Assembly. The Committee handles all
technical matters for the organization. It works closely with
other international agencies interested in safety, such as the
International Telecommunications Union and the International Civil
Aviation Organization, and accomplishes much of its work through
subcommittees which focus upon certain aspects of maritime safety,

such as the carriage of dangerous goods.

The IMCO budget, approved by the Assembly, is borne by all members according to a scale of assessments based on the amount of a state's shipping and trade interests. For example, the United States pays the largest proportion, the United Kingdom the second largest proportion, Norway the third largest proportion, and so forth. The 1978 budget was set at $5,883,400.

THE INTERNATIONAL BANK FOR RECONSTRUCTION AND DEVELOPMENT

The Articles of Agreement which established the International Bank for Reconstruction and Development were drawn up at the Bretton Woods Conference of July, 1944, and the Bank came into legal existence on December 27, 1945. IBRD became a specialized agency of the United Nations in November, 1947, upon the approval of the General Assembly. The first Bank loan was granted in May, 1947. The Bank has as its original purposes¶ to aid in economic reconstruction, due to the damaging effects of World War II; to further the reconversion of wartime economic facilities to peacetime use; to further private enterprise by making loans and guaranteeing loans; and to further international trade and productivity. After an initial concentration on European reconstruction, the Bank moved to the broader role of fostering world-wide economic development. In addition to its lending and guaranteeing operations, the Bank supplies advisory service and other forms of technical assistance. For example, the Bank has helped organize survey missions for various countries to facilitate rational long-range development. The Bank may also lend its good offices to help settle disputes over economic matters between member states. IBRD coordinates programs with FAO, WHO, and UNESCO. It maintains a Staff College and the Economic Development Institute in Washington, D.C. for members. IBRD is affiliated with IDA and IFC. Principal organs of the Bank include the Board of Governors, the Executive Directors, and the President.

The Board of Governors, consisting of one governor appointed by each member state, holds the ultimate power in respect to all phases of the Bank's operations. Governors are appointed for their competence and are frequently former ministers of finance or national bank presidents. The Board meets annually with the Board of Governors of the International Monetary Fund to review operations and establish policy for the Bank. Although most decisions are made by majority vote, voting power is allocated unequally with each Governor receiving 250 votes plus one for each share of Bank stock held by his nation state. This enables the developed states, most notably the United States which holds the preponderance of the stock, to dominate the organization.

There are twenty Executive Directors, five of whom are appointed by the five largest bank shareholders---that is, the United States, the United Kingdom, France, West Germany, and

Japan---with the remainder elected by the governors of the other
member states. The Board of Governors has allocated many of its
responsibilities to the Executive Directors who establish
operating policy for the Bank. Each elected director commands the
votes, as a unit, of the states that have elected him, while
appointed directors cast the votes of the appointing state. Such
a scheme tends to make the voting power of each director more
equal than the voting power of the governors.

The President, elected by the Executive Directors, is the
chief executive officer of the Bank and directs its day-to-day
operations in Washington, D.C. He has the power to appoint and
remove the Bank's staff, consisting of about 2700 persons. The
conditions and terms of IBRD loans are recommended by the
President to the Executive Directors who must approve them. The
President presides over the Executive Directors as chairman and is
entitled to vote only in case of tie. The President meets with
the Board of Governors but may not vote. All Bank presidents have
been US nationals since the Bank's inception.

The membership in the Bank is a privilege of any state which
is a member of the International Monetary Fund. States which
joined the Fund after December 31, 1945 required approval of the
Board of Governors. Membership may be suspended by the Board of
Governors and, if not restored within one year, the suspended
member ceases to be a member of the Bank. The original membership
of twenty-eight states has gradually expanded to 129 in 1978.
Yugoslavia is the only member state with a Communist government.
Cuba withdrew from the organization in November, 1960.

Bank operations are financed, in part, by subscriptions of
member states. The Bank's authorized capital, originally
$10,000,000,000, was raised to $22,948,300,000 in 1967 and is
divided into $100,000 shares, pledged by member states. Two
percent of the total pledge is immediately due, either in gold or
US dollars. Eighteen percent of the pledge (subscription) may be
paid in the member states' own currency and is due upon call.
This fraction along with the original 2% comprises the lending
function of the Bank. The remaining portion of the pledge is
conditionally due, and may be called, should the Bank need it in
order to meet its obligations. Thus far, the Bank has not found
it necessary to make a call for this portion of the subscriptions.
Augmenting the capital of members are the sale of securities and
of some loans, repayment of loans and net earnings as sources of
income. IBRD is entirely self-supporting, with earnings of $238
million for the fiscal year ending June 30, 1978 and reserves of
$2,931 million. At that time, subscribed capital totalled $33,045
million dollars, of which 10% was paid in and 90% was on call.

In addition to these lending sources, the Bank can and does
borrow money and, of course, earns money on its own loans. In
fact, the largest fraction of available funds is obtained from
various private investors, including life insurance companies and
other banks. An administrative budget for the 1978 fiscal year

(IBRD and IDA) was set at $148,126,000.

IBRD loans may be made to governments, political subdivisions of member states, and privately owned economic enterprises within the territory of member states. Loans made to agencies other than a central government, however, must be guaranteed by a central government or a fiscal organ on its behalf.

The Bank is guided in its lending operations by the importance and design of proposed projects, the ability of the borrower to repay, and a condition that the borrower is not able to obtain funds under reasonable conditions from other sources. The terms of the loans depend upon various factors but, particularly, upon the depreciation rate of equipment. Loans up to twenty-five years are frequently made. The interest rate depends, in part, upon the price of money to the Bank itself and, at present, is usually around 6%, 1% of which is a fixed Bank commission.

The Bank has made loans in all geographic areas. Some 1,600 loans were made totalling $44,708.2 million by June 30, 1978 in 105 of the 133 member states.

THE INTERNATIONAL CIVIL AVIATION ORGANIZATION

The International Civil Aviation Organization came into existence on April 4, 1947, in Montreal, Canada, after a sufficient number of ratifications were obtained for the Convention on Civil Aviation (Chicago Convention). The Convention was adopted by the International Civil Aviation Conference of November-December, 1944, attended by fifty-four states. ICAO became a specialized agency of the United Nations in May, 1947, and reports to the Economic and Social Council.

The major purpose of ICAO is to promote international civil aviation, with an emphasis on safety and economy. To accomplish this objective, ICAO: (1) fosters air passage by encouraging state cooperation, planning and joint support of air facilities, such as weather reporting stations; (2) fosters the preparation of conventions on air traffic matters---such as the Convention on the International Recognition of Rights on Aircraft, adopted by the IACO Assembly in June, 1948; (3) settles disputes between members in respect to the Chicago Convention; (4) establishes binding rules and makes recommendations concerning various aspects of air traffic; (5) provides legal and training services under the UN Development Program; and (6) announces the Edward Warner Award annually. Library fellowships are also available through ICAO. ICAO has successfully implemented international standards of air traffic safety and control, communications and navigation facilities. Any member unable to conform must notify ICAO, which publishes the results. International standards are constantly being updated and revised due to changes in air technology. For example, the problems of hijacking, air piracy, and aircraft noise were recently addressed by the ICAO.

The principal organs of ICAO are the Assembly, Council, and Secretary-General. The organization regularly publishes the ICAO Bulletin and Memorandum on ICAO as well as a number of technical, legal and economic documents.

Each member state has the right to representation in the Assembly and possesses one vote. The Assembly convenes at least once every three years. Most decisions require a simple majority, although an amendment to the Chicago Convention requires a two-thirds majority vote. The Assembly may specify which states' ratifications are necessary before an amendment comes into force and the Assembly possesses the power to deny ICAO membership to a state which refuses to ratify an amendment adopted by the Assembly. In 1971 the Assembly denied South Africa the right to participate in ICAO meetings. Other powers and activities of the Assembly include: (1) election of Council members; (2) determination of the budget; (3) recommendation of policy to the Council and member states; (4) submission of reports to the Economic and Social Council of the United Nations; (5) consideration of any matter referred to it by the Council.

The Council consists of thirty member states elected for three-year terms by the Assembly. Geographic factors, contribution to air navigation facilities and importance in air traffic matters influence the choice of council members. The Council carries on the work of the organization by meeting continuously. An important function of the Council is the preparation of binding standards. The Council is assisted in this task by the Air Navigation Commission, consisting of fifteen experts and three observers appointed by the Council, whose recommended standards approved by the Council are submitted to member states. Unless a majority of member states reject a standard, it automatically becomes part ot the Convention and, therefore, is binding on all member states, regardless of their approval. Council recommendations go through the same procedures but are not considered legally binding. Nevertheless, they are considered policy lines that member states are obligated to attempt to conform to. In addition to the Commission, the Council is also assisted by the Air Transportation Committee, the COmmittee on Joint Support of Air Navigation Services, and the Financial Committee. All members of these Committees are appointed by the Council. The Council is also empowered to decide disputes between member states if negotiations fail and one party brings the dispute to the Council. The Council has the right to call upon member states to deny air space to airlines defying the Convention and to deny voting rights to members in case of violations. In addition, the Council possesses broad investigatory powers. The US recently urged and obtained the upgrading of standards in order to prevent air crimes.

The Secretary-General is appointed by the Council for a five-year term and supervises, under the direction of the Council, the staff on ICAO, consisting of approximately 827 persons located

in Montreal. The Secretariat services the other organs by
performing technical, clerical, and informational functions.
    The regular budget is established by the Assembly. Member
states are assessed according to their ability to pay. The United
States is responsible for approximately one-third of the regular
budget. ICAO also receives United Nations monies because of its
participation in the United Nations Development Program. The 1978
budget amounted to $22,823,000.
    The Chicago Convention allows World War II allies and
neutrals to join the Organization simply by ratification of the
Convention. Other states must obtain a four-fifths vote of
acceptance by the ICAO Assembly and a majority vote of the General
Assembly of the United Nations. One hundred and forty-three
states are members, including certain Communist states, e.g.,
Czechoslovakia, Poland, Yugoslavia, Bulgaria, Cambodia, China,
Cuba, Hungary, Laos, Romania, USSR, and Vietnam.

THE INTERNATIONAL DEVELOPMENT ORGANIZATION

    IDA came into existence on September 24, 1960, as an
affiliate of the International Bank for Reconstruction and
Development, after a sufficient nember of Bank members had
accepted its Articles of Agreement.   The Association's basic
purpose is to promote the economic development of underdeveloped
member states. This is done by a more lenient and flexible
financing of projects for underdeveloped states than would be the
case if they financed with the International Bank for
Reconstruction and Development. Credits may be granted to such
states on an interest free, fifty-year repayment plan (although
there is a .75% per annum service charge), in contrast to IBRD's
approximately 6% interest rate (including commission) and seven to
twenty-five year repayment period. Also, arrangements can be made
for loans through IDA with no repayment for the first ten years.
    The principal organs of the IDA are the Board of Governors,
the Executive-Director, and the President.
    The Board of Governors of IDA is the same, and performs the
same functions, as the Board of Governors of IBRD. When voting on
IDA matters the voting power of a governor is basically
proportional to his state's subscription to IDA. The US governor,
for example, commands approximately 30% of all the votes. The
annual Board Meeting is in September.
    The Executive Directors of IDA are also the Executive
Directors of IBRD with similar functions and voting arrangements.
    The President of IDA also serves as the President of IBRD.
The various officers and staff below him service IDA in the same
way as the Bank.
    IDA's operations are financed primarily through member's
subscriptions and certain supplementary contributions made by
economically more advanced states. The amount of IDA
subscriptions is based upon the amount of subscriptions to IBRD.

More advanced states are designated as Part I members and pay
their subscriptions in a convertible form over a five-year period.
Less developed members are designated as Part II members and are
allowed to pay 90% of their subscription in their national
currency and the remaining 10% in convertible currency over a
five-year period. Part II members have the right to deny IDA
credit grants involving their own currency. IDA also enjoys
grants from World Bank income and from income of its own, in
addition to the subscriptions of members, particularly its 21
wealthiest members.

By the end of 1979, IDA had development credits totalling
$18,062,000,000. India has been the largest recipient of IDA aid,
receiving nearly half of the credits granted. The 1979 fiscal
year administrative budget was $148,126,000. IDA has granted 765
credits totalling $13,710 million to 69 of the less developed
nations.

Membership is open to any state which is a member of the
International Bank for Reconstruction and Development. As of
January, 1980, IDA had 120 members. IDA headquarters are located
in Wasington, D.C., with regional offices in London, Paris and
Tokyo. IDA publishes Finance and Development (quarterly),
memorandums on policies and operations, and an annual report.

THE INTERNATIONAL FINANCE CORPORATION

The International Finance Corporation, founded on July 20,
1956, is affiliated with, but legally separate from, the
International Bank for Reconstruction and Development. The
primary function of the Corporation is to further economic
enterprise in underdeveloped nations. This is accomplished by IFC
investment in cooperation with private capital in various
projects, such as mining and manufacturing, where private capital
is insufficient. Private investment is also faclitated through
research and information dissemination concerning possible
economic opportunities and the soundness of projects. Investments
are limited to private enterprises located within member states.
Member governments need not guarantee repayment of investments to
the Corporation in projects concerning their nationals. A member
government, however, may prevent investments in its jurisdiction
by IFC. As a specialized agency of the United Nations, the
Corporation reports to the Economic and Social Council. Its
principal organs are the Board of Governors, the Board of
Directors, and the President.

The Board of Governors is composed of the governors of the
International Bank for Reconstruction and Development whose
countries hold mebership in IFC. The functions of the Board are
similar to those of IBRD and meetings are held simultaneously with
board meetings of the Bank and the International Development
Association.

The Board of Directors of IFC consist of those directors of

the International Bank for Reconstruction and Development
representing countries that belong to IFC. The Board plays the
same role as it does in the case of IBRD and elects the President
of IFC.

The President of IFC, elected by the Board of Directors,
plays the same role as the President of the International Bank for
Reconstruction and Development. In fact, the same person has
served both positions. In contrast to the International
Development Association, however, IFC has a small but separate
staff from that of IBRD.

Membership in IFC is an optional privilege of the members of
the International Bank for Reconstruction and Development. One
hundred eight of the Bank members have become members of the
Corporation.

The operations of IFC are financed through subscriptions made
by member states, earnings from investments, and borrowed funds.
Capital is authorized at $107,000,000, with reserves of
$54,000,000. As in the case of the International Bank for
Reconstruction and Development, the size of the country's
subscription determines its voting power. Thus, the United
States, with the largest subscription, commands approximately 30%
of the total vote. By the end of the fiscal year 1978, IFC's
activities embraced gross total commitments of over $2,103 million
with projects in 67 countries. A recent administrative budget was
set at $10,000,000 to be met from income. Members' subscriptions
reached $144 million on June 30, 1978, with reserves of $140.1
million. IFC has made loans totalling $2,103 million to 75
nations.

THE INTERNATIONAL LABOR ORGANIZATION

ILO was created in 1919 by the Treaty of Versailles as an
autonomous organization associated with the League of Nations. In
1946, after constitutional amendments, it became the first
specialized agency of the United Nations reporting to the Economic
and Social Council. ILO's basic purpose is to further social
justice as a contribution to international peace. ILO's
constitution specifies concern with numerous matters including
hours of work, unemployment, workers' health, child labor, old-age
security, freedom of association, and educational matters. The
aims of the organization were further specified in the Declaration
of Philadelphia, adopted at an ILO conference in 1944. This
declaration includes concern with standards of living, fitting
persons to occupations, labor mobility, policy development in
respect to hours and wages, extending the right of collective
bargaining, equality of opportunity, and problems connected with
nutrition, housing, recreation, and child welfare. A primary
concern of ILO is to establish an International Labor Code. In
addition, ILO renders various types of services and technical
assistance.

The principal organs are the International Labor Conference, the Governing Body, and the Director-General (International Labor Office).

The International Labor Conference, which meets yearly at Geneva, is the basic policy-making organ of ILO and consists of four voting delegates from each member state. The delegates are appointed so that two of them represent the member government, one represents the employers, and one represents the workers of a member state. The selection of employers' and workers' representatives are made by member governments in consultation with representative organizations of workers and employers. For example, when the US was a member, the US Chamber of Commerce and the National Association of Manufacturers approved the employers' representative and the AFL-CIO approved the worker's representative. During the Conference, delegates divide along governmental, employer, and worker lines for organizational and certain elective purposes. The primary work of the Conference is to establish an International Labor Code which consists of Conventions adopted by the Conference effective after state ratification. Member governments are obligated to submit each convention to the ratification process, even though it may not be successfully ratified. Recommendations that have legislative implications must be submitted by member governments to appropriate organs for possible action. Member governments are also obligated to report to ILO on the implementation of the conventions and recommendations. A Commission of Inquiry may hear complaints concerning failure of a state to live up to a convention that it has ratified.

One of the primary problems of the Conference has been to adjust its requirements that employers be represented due to the fact that a number of member states no longer have private employers, because of extensive nationalization (i.e., Communist states).

The Governing Body is the principal executive organ of ILO consisting of fifty-six members---twenty-eight of whom represent governments, fourteen of whom represent employers, and fourteen of which represent workers. Ten governments of primary industrial importance are permanently represented. These are: Canada, China, France, West Germany, India, Italy, Japan, USSR, and the United Kingdom. Nonpermanent governmental members are elected by permanent governmental representatives. The employer and worker members are elected by their respective groups in the International Labor Conference, excepting those representatives whose governents have permanent seats. The Governing Body normally meets three or four times a year and appoints the Director-General; makes preparations for the Labor Conference, including agenda composition; and reviews the budget prior to its submission to the Conference. (The budget is initially drawn up by the Director-General.) The Governing Body is also concerned with policy directives to the International Labor Office.

The Director-General appointed by the Governing Body is the chief executive officer of ILO, playing a role similar to the Secretary-General of the United Nations, with responsibility for the recruitment and appointment of his staff, who service the various organs of ILO in a secretarial and technical fashion and carry out programs determined by the International Labor Conference and the Governing Body. The International Labor Office is headed by the Director General, who arranges for meetings, gathers and publicizes information, conducts studies required by the Conference or the Governing Body and, on request, advises member governments. There are approximately 2800 staff members, including 900 technical experts in the field. The Director-General is also responsible for the Annual Report which provides a discussion focal point for the yearly International Labor Conference.

The International Labor Code consists of over 310 conventions and recommendations which have been adopted by the International Labor Conference. Conventions are binding upon states that have accepted them. Should a worker or employer organization feel that a particular convention is not being applied, they may file a complaint with the International Labor Office. The Governing Body may then decide to publish the facts of the case for the scrutiny of other members. Should a member state feel that another member state has violated a convention, a Commission of Inquiry may examine the matter and make recommendations. Although states are not bound by recommendations and unratified conventions, nevertheless, they are bound to give information to the Governing Body concerning the reasons why ratification of a Conference-adopted convention has not been completed and in cases where there has been a failure to implement Conference recommendations, the reasons for nonimplementation. The Code covers a wide variety of matters including treatment of migrants, maximum hours or work, holidays, old-age insurance, contract clauses, rights of association, and minimum wages.

The principal source of revenue for the Organization is members states who are assessed using a scale of contributions applied to a yearly budget ($169,000,000 was approved for 1978-79). ILO also receives funds by participating in the United Nations Development Program.

Membership in ILO is optional. This option may be exercised by United Nations members by notification of the Director-General of ILO. The bulk of the United Nations members, including Communist states, are presently members of ILO.

On November 5, 1975 the US gave notice that it planned to leave the organization unless measures were taken to return it to its original goals. The US, in particular, cited four reasons for its original goals. The US, in particular, cited four reasons for its concern: (1) ILO failure to apply the same labor standards to all member countries equally; (2) formal condemnations effected without exhaustive investigation of problems; (3) non-political labor matters infused with political concerns; and (4) ILO

departure from its original goals. On November 1, 1977 the US
announced its official withdrawal from the organization, and
indicated plans to return when the ILO returned to "its proper
principles and procedures." Since the US has contributed 25% of
the ILO budget, the threat of its departure might set an important
precedent for other nations which have shared US sentiments. On
February 18, 1980, however, the US reversed its previous decision
and re-joined the ILO as a full functioning member.

There are currently 136 members in the ILO. The central
headquarters are located in Geneva, with branch offices in cities
such as London, Rio de Janeiro, Rome, and Washington. ILO is
responsible for numerous publications, many of a technical nature
concerning such matters as unemployment, wages, prices, etc. It
also publishes a monthly International Labor Review, a quarterly
magazine entitled I.L.O. News, and a yearly summary of statistics
entitled Yearbook of Labor Statistics.

THE INTERNATIONAL MONETARY FUND

The International Monetary Fund came into existence on
December 27, 1945, when a sufficient number of states had ratified
its Articles of Agreement. The Articles were drawn up by the
United Nations Monetary and Financial Conference (Bretton Woods
Conference) of July, 1944. IMF became a specialized agency of the
United Nations in November, 1947, and reports to the Economic and
Social Council.

IMF's primary purposes are to foster international monetary
cooperation, international trade, and exchange stability. It does
this by establishing a multilateral system of payments to assist
in the elimination of foreign exchange restrictions and by
attempting to promote currency stability by making Fund resources
available to members under suitable safeguards. In addition, the
organization provides technical advice and assistance to members
in respect to monetary matters.

Recently, considerable progress in the establishment of a
multilateral system of payments has been made because a number of
members have accepted obligations under Article VIII, which limits
restrictive innovations in respect to exchange rates and currency
practices upon consent of the IMF.

One of the most important services of the Fund is to allow
members to charge purchases of one another's currency. This
promotes currency stability and helps adjust for temporary
imbalances in the payments situation. Ratification of the Second
Amendment to the Articles of Agreement, on April 1, 1978 increased
the power of the Managing Director who supervises national
exchange rate policies.

The principal organs of the Fund are the Board of Governors,
the Executive Directors, and the Managing Director.

Each member state is entitled to one governor and one
alternate governor on the Board of Governors. The function of the

alternate governor is to act for the governor in his absence.
Each governor wields 250 votes plus additional votes, depending
upon the size of his country's contribution to IMF resources.
This system gives the developed states a dominant voice in the
organization. For example, the US governor commands something
over 20% of the vote, the United Kingdom's governor around 12%,
Western Germany's governor 4%, and so forth. The Board normally
meets once a year and decides most questions by a simple majority
vote. Although the Articles of Agreement place all power over IMF
affairs in the hands of the Board, in practice, the Executive
Directors make most of the important decisions.

The Executive Directors decide upon policy in respect to the
operations of the Fund. The United States, the United Kingdom,
Western Germany, France, Saudi Arabia, and Japan, by virtue of the
size of their quota of IMF, are each allowed to appoint one
director. The remaining fifteen directors are elected by the
Board of Governors. Each elected director casts the votes of
those states which elected him. The Directors meet as the
occasion requires and are considered as being in continuous
session. Numerous technical decisions, such as those concerning
convertibility, constitute a large portion of the Executive
Directors' work load.

The Managing Director is the principal executive officer of
the Fund. He executes the policy of the Executive Directors and
the Board of Governors. The Director is elected for a five-year
term by the Executive Directors and is in charge of a staff of
1,250 persons drawn from member states on the basis of merit and
wide geographic distribution. The staff is responsible for
handling the business of the Fund, which includes research,
consultation, and publication activities.

Administrative costs for 1979 ($75,000,000) were met from
earnings by a budget approved by the Board of Governors. Income
from charges and returns from investments normally exceed these
costs. Fund operations, on the other hand, utilize Fund resources
derived from subscriptions from member states, based upon quotas.
Quotas for original members were initially set in the Articles of
Agreement at the Bretton Woods Conference. The Board of Governors
establishes quotas for other states as they come in to IMF.
Quotas may be revised by a four-fifths vote of the Board of
Governors and become effective upon the consent of those members
who together subscribe two-thirds of the total quota amount.
Members are required to pay 25% of their quota in gold and the
remaining 75% in their national currency. This is the case unless
this requirement forces a state to divest itself of more than 10%
of its net dollar-gold holdings. In such a case, the state
concerned pays up to the 10% limit and then meets the remainder of
its quota with its own national currency. The effect of this rule
is to allow poorer states to pay a greater proportion of their
quota in their own currency.

All Fund member currencies are expressed in terms of US

dollars and/or gold. Once a par value has been agreed upon between a member state and the Fund, significant manipulations of it by a member state must be consented to by the Fund or the member will lose its membership rights in respect to the Fund's operations. This arrangement is intended to curtail the type of harmful practices which occurred in the 1930's when states attempted to gain an economic advantage through unilateral devaluation.

The headquarters are located in Washington, D.C. with regional offices in Geneva and Paris. IMF publications include: International Financial Statistics, Balance of Payments Yearbook, International Financial News Survey, and an Annual Report. The Fund has negotiated agreements with ten of its most advanced industrial members to lend up to $6 billion to correct or prevent serious disruptions of the international monetary system. In February, 1978, IMF completed its seventh review of quotas, which directly affect the drawing rights of members. It also dealt with: (1) the special drawing right; (2) gold sales; and (3) Fund surveillance.

THE INTERNATIONAL TELECOMMUNICATIONS UNION

The International Telecommunications Union, formed by the International Telecommunications Convention of 1934, replaced the International Telegraph Union, formed by the Paris Convention of 1865. The Telecommunication Convention was drastically revised in 1947 at which time the ITU became a specialized agency of the United Nations. The structural innovations of the 1947 revisions became effective January 1, 1949. Additional revisions were made after the Buenos Aires Plenipotentiary Conference of 1952, the Geneva Conference of 1959, and the Montreux Conference of 1965. The latter revisions became effective January 1,1967. ITU revised the Convention again in 1973.

The organization's major purpose is to foster the rational use of telecommunications media and to promote state cooperation on such matters. To further these objectives, the Union: (1) makes studies and disseminates information; (2) provides training and technical assistance; (3) registers frequencies for individual stations to foster maximum rational use; and (4) allocates frequencies in respect to categories of use---such as maritime, meteorlogical and coastal.

On October 23, 1973 ITU revised the International Telecommunications Convention, including such matters as radio frequencies, cost rates, survival via telecommunications and research studies.

The principal organs of ITU are the Plenipotentiary Conference, the Administrative Conferences, the Administrative Council, the International Frequency Registration Board, two Consultative Committees for Radio and for Telegraph, and the Secretary-General (Secretariat).

All members may participate in the Plenipotentiary Conference, but only full members are entitled to vote. The Plenipotentiary Conference meets irregularly but meets at least once every five years. It determines the general policy of the organization, receives and considers the report of the Administrative Council, elects the members of the Administrative Concil and the Secretary-General, adopts revisions to the Telecommunications Convention, and sets the upward limit on the expenses of the organization.

Administrative Conferences deal with a particular communications area, particularly to consider revisions of the regulations which are annexed to the Telecommunications Convention. Two conferences in which all members participate, one dealing with telegraph and telephone matters and the other with radio, normally meet close to the time of the Plenipotentiary Conference. The members of the Radio Conference supervise the work of the International Frequency Registration Board.

The Administrative Council consists of thirty-six members elected by the Plenipotentiary Conference to act on its behalf between conference meetings. The Council normally meets once a year and supervises the activities of the Secretary-General, the International Frequency Registration Board, and the Consultative Committees. The Council approves the annual budget in terms of guidelines laid down by the Plenipotentiary Conference and reports to the Conference.

The five members of the International Frequency Board are elected by the Administrative Radio Conference, as technical experts with the primary function of recording broadcasting frequency usages. Also, the members provide technical advice, disseminate information, and may make certain types of investigations concerning the use of frequencies. The primary objective of the Board is to maximize the utilization of the broadcasting frequency spectrum.

Two Consultative Committees---specifically, the International Telegraphic and Telephone Consultative Committee and the International Radio Consultative Committee---study problems of a technical nature connected with tariffs, operations, safety, transmission, and circuitry. Members of interested international and private organizations are members of these committees as well as representatives of states. Much of the work is accomplished through study groups which report to the Plenary Sessions of the committees, which normally meet every three years. The reports form the basis of technical recommendations made to members in the hope of fostering cooperation and the rational utilization of facilities.

The states that were present at the Bretton Woods Conference of 1944 possessed the right of membership if they ratified the Articles of Agreement prior to December 31, 1945. Membership since then has been open to any state which, after application, can secure a simple majority of the total votes cast by the Board

of Governors. The present membership (154) includes the bulk of
United Nations members and certain non-United Nations member
states.

The annual budget, set for 1978 at $60,600,000, is borne by
the ITU members who contribute varying amounts in terms of a
voluntary classification scheme which sets the amount of
contribution. Generally speaking, the large states pay
considerably less, as a fraction of total assessments, than in the
case of the other specialized agencies.

The permanent headquarters are in Geneva, Switzerland. The
Union publishes numerous materials, many of a highly technical
nature such as lists of telephone routes and circuits, as well as
a less technical monthly journal.

THE UNIVERSAL POSTAL UNION

The first International Postal Congress met in 1874--in
Bern---and established, through the International Postal
Convention, the General Postal Union. The second congress, held
in 1878, renamed the organization the Universal Postal Union.
Various postal congresses, held prior to World War II, extended
and amended the Convention. In 1947, the Postal Congress held in
Paris amended the Convention to make UPU a specialized agency of
the United Nations, upon agreement of the General Assembly.
Subsequent postal congresses have further altered the Convention
with the provisions adopted at the Vienna Congress of 1964,
presently effecive.

The basic purpose of the Union is to perfect postal services
within the area embraced by the Union and to promote international
cooperation in respect to such services. To further these
objectives, the Union: engages in research; provides technical
assistance; arbitrates disputes between member states concerning
regulations; and facilitates the settling of financial accounts
generated by international postal services.

The principal organs are: the Universal Postal Congress, the
Executive and Liaison Committee, the Consultative Commission on
Postal Studies, and the Secretary-General (International Bureau).

The Congress consists of all UPU members, each entitled to one
vote. It has as its primary function the review and modification
of the Universal Postal Convention. The entire territory of the
member states is viewed as a "single territory" to which the
Convention applies for all ordinary mail, such as letters,
postcards, commercial papers, etc. All members are bound to apply
the uniform standards established by the Convention within the
territory. Other services---such as C.O.D., money orders, insured
letters, and parcel post---are covered by special agreements which
bind only those members which adhere to them. In addition to work
on the Convention, the Congress elects the Executive and Liaison
Committee and reviews the functions of the organization. Although
the Congress meets irregularly, it must meet at least once every

five years.

The Executive Council (before 1965, the Executive and Liaison Committee) consists of forty members elected by the Congress. The Council provides continuity between Congresses. In this capacity, it supervises the work of the International Bureau and appoints its Director, maintains relationships with other international organizations, makes studies, and provides technical information to members. It also reviews possible revisions in the Postal Convention and makes recommendations to the Congress.

The Consultative Committee for Postal Studies was created by the Ottawa Conference of 1957 for the purpose of carrying out studies and rendering technical advice on various aspects of postal service. Each member of UPU is a member of the Committee, although a thirty-five-member Consultative Council on Postal Studies (previously the Management Council) coordinates and directs the work. In 1966, the Council undertook studies of mechanization and automation of accounting, technological advances in postal services of developing countries, and methods of reaching staff requirements in post offices.

The Director-General of the International Bureau is appointed by the Executive and Liaison Committee and heads a small staff (approximately 130) at the headquarters in Bern. The Bureau is responsible for: liaison work with member states and other organizations; information gathering and dissemination; various service arrangements; and the settling of accounts between states in respect to their postal services.

The UPU has 158 members. Prior to 1947, any state wishing to become a member of the Union could do so by accession to the Universal Postal Convention. Since that time, new applicants, after notifying the Swiss government, must be approved by a two-thirds absolute majority of UPU members. The Union embraces most states, including communist ones, as members. On June 5, 1964, South Africa was expelled from UPU by the UPU Congress. South Africa's expulsion was controversial because it related to the practice of apartheid rather than the violation of UPU regulations.

Member states meet ordinary, annual expenses through a contributions classification scheme ranging from one to seven, whereby the lower the class the higher the assessment due. The classification of a particular member is determined by the Swiss government in agreement with the government concerned. For example, Canada, France, India, New Zealand, United Kingdom, and the United States fall into class one, while the Ivory Coast, Iceland, and Mali fall into class seven. Maximum annual expenditures are established by each Congress. A 1978 budget was estimated at $11,714,000. Income from the sale of documents and certain other sources also helps defray expenses.

The organization is responsible for numerous publications such as the Universal Postal Convention, the Postal Union and UPU: Its Foundation and Development.

THE WORLD HEALTH ORGANIZATION

The World Health Organization came into legal existence on
April 7, 1948, after twenty-six states had ratified its
constitution and became functional on September 1 of the same
year. WHO's constitution was formed and adopted by the
International Health Conference of June-July, 1946, sponsored by
the Economic and Social Council of the United Nations. WHO
absorbed the assets and functions of the League Health
Organization and the International Office of Public Health and
transformed some regional sanitary bureaus, possessing prior,
separate existences, into regional offices. The Organization's
basic purpose is to promote the highest possible level of health
by coordinating international health work, conducting and
promoting research, gathering and disseminating information,
providing technical assistance and services, establishing and
promoting standardization procedures and nomenclature, and
proposing agreements and conventions on international health
matters.
The principal organs are the World Health Assembly, the
Executive Board, and the Director (Secretariat).
The World Health Assembly, which meet annually, normally in
Geneva, consists of delegates from member states with each member
possessing one vote. The Assembly establishes the basic policy
and programs of the organization, approves the budget, appoints
the Director-General, elects the Executive Board, and adopts, by a
two-thirds vote, conventions and regulations. Conventions, if
accepted through proper constitutional procedures by member
states, become binding upon the signatories. Each state is
obligated to submit Assembly-adopted conventions to its
constitutional processes within eighteen months of adoption.
State ratifying organs concerned, however, are not under more than
a moral obligation to ratify the conventions. Regulations adopted
by the Assembly are binding on all states except those who object
to the regulations within a certain time period. It is normal to
consider a particular health problem of world-wide importance at
each annual conference. For example, the 1967 conference made the
eradication of smallpox its main target. In 1970, WHO reported
that the incidence of smallpox had been reduced by an estimated
70%. Following the outbreak of cholera among victims of the
India-Pakistan War, attention was focused in 1971 on that disease.
The new emphasis for the decade of the seventies appeared to be
environmental factors, with the interest on smoking predominant at
the 1972 meeting, during which it was also resolved to ban smoking
at all WHO conferences.
In January,1980, WHO scored a tremendous triumph and reached a
long dreamed of goal when it announced the complete eradication of
smallpox from the face of the earth.
The Executive Board consists of thirty qualified individuals,
designated by member states elected by the World Health Assembly,

following the rule of equitable geographic distribution. Persons so designated operate in terms of the dictates of their technical competence rather than as delegates of the appointing states. The Board normally meets twice a year but may hold special sessions. The primary function of the Board is to supervise the execution of the policies decided upon by the Assembly. Also, it is authorized to take certain emergency measures in unusual circumstances, acting through the Director-General and his Secretariat.

The Director-General, appointed by the Assembly, heads the Secretariat, composed of a technical and administrative staff of about 3500 persons. A sizeable portion of the work at the central headquarters in Geneva consists of coordinating the very active regional offices. In fact, over two-thirds of the staff working on behalf of WHO are located somewhere other than at the central headquarters. The members of the Secretariat engage in a wide variety of functions including technical assistance, information collection and dissemination, and various services.

Members of the United Nations may become members of WHO by accepting the WHO constitution and giving notification of this fact to the Secretary-General of the United Nations. States that are not members of the United Nations may be admitted, after application, upon acceptance by the World Health Assembly (majority vote). Certain entities that are not full states may be admitted by the Assembly as associate members. By January, 1972, the Organization had 151 full members, including the Communist states of the United Nations.

WHO finances its various functions through voluntary contributions, participation in the United Nations Development Program, and a regular budget. Each member pays a portion of the regular budget according to a scale of contributions. For example, the United States' share is approximately 30%, the Soviet Union's share approximately 14%, and the United Kingdom's share approximately 7%. A current budget was set at $165,000,000.

The permanent headquarters are in Geneva, Switzerland, but much of the work is done in the regional offices. The six regional health offices are located at Brazzaville, for Africa; New Delhi, for Southeast Asia; Copenhagen, for Europe; Alexandria, for the eastern Meditarranean; Manila, for the western Pacific; and Washington, D.C. for the Americas. The Organization is responsible for a large number of diverse materials including¶ Bulletin of the World Health Organization, Chronicle of World Health Organization, World Health, and Weekly Epidemiological Record.

THE WORLD METEOROLOGICAL ORGANIZATION

WMO came into formal existence in March, 1950, after thirty states had ratified the World Meteorological Convention which had been adopted by a Conference of Directors of national meteorological services held in Washington, D.C., in 1947. WMO was preceeded by the International Meteorological Organization (IMO), created in 1878 by a conference held at Utrecht, Netherlands. IMO consisted of an association of the directors of national meteorological sevices and was not viewed as constituting an intergovernmantal organization until 1939 when states, rather than directors, became members. After the acceptance of the 1947 WMO Convention, the functions and assets of IMO were absorbed by WMO and the latter became a specialized agency of the United Nations, reporting to the Economic and Social Council. The basic purposes of WMO are to promote: the establishment of meteorological stations and centers; the creation of systems of weather information exchange; the standardization of procedures and nomenclature; the application of weather information to the various human activities such as aviation and shipping; and the further research and training activities connected with meteorology. In addition, WMO may make recommendations to states, propose conventions, and perform research and technical assistance. Its major concern at the present time is the World Weather Watch, an international effort directed at the provision of better weather forecasting, the gaining further knowledge of the atmosphere, and the assessment of damage to the atmosphere by the use of technology. The principal organs are the Congress, the Executive Committee, and the Secretary-General (Secretariat).

The WMO Congress is the primary policy-making body of the organization, consisting of delegates (directors of meteorological services) of members. Each member possesses one vote, with a simple majority deciding elections and a two-thirds majority of those voting deciding other questions. An important function of the Congress is the adoption of technical regulations pertaining to meteorological practices. In addition, the Congress elects the President, two Vice-Presidents, and members of the Executive Committee. The World Meteorological Convention requires that the Assembly meet at least once every four years. Presently, there are 147 members in the Congress.

The Congress of WMO has established eight technical Commissions composed of experts, to engage in technical studies of areas such as aeronautical meteorology, maritime meteorology, and agricultural meteorology. The commissions make recommendations, usually concerning procedures and technical regulations, to the Executive Committee and to the WMO Congress. The meetings of the Executive Committee and the Congress are attended by the officers of the commissions, who may participate but not vote in these bodies.

The Executive Committee consists of twenty-four directors of national meteorological services and automatically includes WMO's President, the two Vice-Presidents, and the presidents of the Regional Associations. The remaining members are elected by the Congress. The Committee makes decisions by a two-thirds majority vote and operates, basically, to carry out policies determined by the WMO Congress. It also engages in studies, advises members,

and makes recommendations to the Congress. Members of the
Executive Committee act as individuals and, therefore, do not
represent nations.

Regional Associations are organizations of the members
---e.g., Africa, Asia, South America, North and Central America,
the Southwest Pacific and Europe. They meet when necessary and
foster cooperation among their members, particularly in respect to
information exchange and the maintenance of meteorological
stations. They also perform functions based on the resolutions of
the WMO Congress and examine, from a regional perspective,
questions submitted to them by the Executive Committee. The
president of each Regional Association is automatically a member
of the Executive Committee.

The Secretary-General heads a small staff in Geneva and
operates under the direction of the Executive Committee and the
WMO Congress. The secretariat functions as a communications
center, engages in technical studies, performs secretarial
services for other organs, and is responsible for publications.

Applicants (not necessarily states) which maintain separate
meteorological services are potential members of WMO. Entities
which attended the 1947 WMO conference and members of the United
Nations can become members of WMO simply by adhering to the WMO
Convention. Other entities may become members, upon application,
if approved by two-thirds of the members of the organization. By
September, 1978, the bulk (147) of the world's potentially
acceptable applicants had become members, including many Communist
states. The Communist states of Vietnam and North Korea, however,
are not members. South Africa was suspended in April, 1975.

A regular four-year budget is approved by the WMO Congress
and is paid by the members according to a scale of assessments
established by the Congress. The scale of assessments reflects
ability to pay, with the United States paying the highest portion,
the USSR the second highest portion, the United Kingdom the third
highest portion, and so forth. The 1976-79 budget amounted to
$40,542,000. WMO also receives monies as a participant in the
United Nations Development Program and acts as an executing agency
for meteorological projects connected with the United Nations
Special Fund.

WMO is resposible for a variety of technical publications
including a quarterly WMO Bulletin. The permanent headquarters
are in Geneva, Switzerland.

United Nations Educational, Scientific, and Cultural Organization

UNESCO came into existence (November 4, 1946) after twenty
states had ratified its constitution, which had been adopted by a
conference held in London in November, 1945, attended by
forty-four states. The Organization entered into a relationship
with the United Nations, in December, 1946, as a specialized
agency, reporting to the Economic and Social Council. UNESCO's

basic purposes are to contribute to peace and security by
fostering cooperation in the educational, scientific, and cultural
fields, and to promote respect for justice, the rules of law, and
fundamental rights and freedoms irrespective of race, sex,
language, or religious differences. In this connection, it
functions to promote exchanges of persons, artifacts, and
publications; the development of educational facilities; and the
preservation of books, art works, and cultural artifacts. UNESCO
has the right to recommend conventions to states, engage in
research, and participate in various regional and world
development programs, i.e., currently one to write an eight volume
General History of Africa. In such activities, it renders a wide
variety of informational and technical services. UNESCO recently
conducted a worldwide historic preservation campaign. Thus,
UNESCO frequently provides facts that are necessary to get a
perspective on the basic world problems. Recently, for example,
UNESCO noted that the world illiteracy rate was about thirty-four
percent, a substantial reduction from the nearly fifty percent
rate of 1950.

The basic organs of UNESCO are the General Conference, the
Executive Board, and the Director-General (Secretariat).

The Director-General is the chief executive officer and is
responsible for UNESCO's program and Secrtariat staff of about
3,500 persons. He is nominated by the Executive Board and
appointed for a six-year term by the General Conference. Under
the supervision of the Executive Board, he appoints and dismisses
members of his staff (144) and is responsible for budget estimates
and the UNESCO work program.

The General Conference, presently meeting once every two
years, consists of delegates from member states and determines
basic UNESCO policy. Although each member may send up to five
delegates to the conference, all members possess but one vote.
Member states are required by the UNESCO constitution to consult
with national UNESCO commissions, when established, and various
national educational, scientific, and cultural organizations in
the selection of delegates.

Most Conference recommendations require only a simple majority
vote, although a two-thirds majority vote is required for: (1)
admission of new members, (2) the adoption of an international
convention, and (3) the approval of observers from other
international organizations and nongovernmental organizations.
When the Conference adopts conventions, members are required to
submit them for possible ratification within one year after the
close of the session. Members are also required to have competent
authorities consider Conference recommendations. Also,
international conferences, relating to UNESCO's field of concern,
may be summoned by the Conference.

National Commissions are organized groups of persons, normally
specialists within the fields of education, science, and culture,
formed within member states for the purposes of furthering UNESCO

ends by advising delegations to the General Conference and their own governments. They also perform various publication, liaison, and public relations tasks. Although National Commissions are not required by the UNESCO constitution, each member state is requested to form such commissions and the majority of UNESCO members have done so.

In 1979 UNESCO convened in order to consider a resolution from the USSR that governments be responsible for all mass media within their borders. This move was viewed as censorship by the West. A Third World news agency was being planned, which UNESCO viewed as offsetting the "cultural and economic imperialism" of Western wire services.

Membership in UNESCO is open to all United Nations members. Non-United Nations members must gain the recommendation of the Executive Board and approval (two-thirds majority) of the General Conference. Switzerland, North and South Korea, and Monaco (as non-UN members) have been admitted under the latter procedure. Entities which are not responsible under international law, may be admitted as "associate members," but they are not allowed to vote. There are presently 144 full members and two associate members, the British East Carribbean Group and Namibia.

The Executive Board consists of 45 members. It prepares the program to be submitted to the Conference and supervises its execution. It meets two or three times a year.

After a two-year budget has been approved by the General Conference, member states are assessed, as in the case of the United Nations, using a scale of contributions based upon ability to pay. The United States' share is approximately thirty percent; the USSR, fifteen percent; and so forth. In addition, UNESCO receives United Nations monies to cover the cost of its role in the United Nations Development Program. Expenditures have constantly moved upward. A recent budget amounted to $236.2 million.

UNESCO headquarters are located in Paris with regional training centers for Latin America in Mexico and for Arabs, in Egypt. Additionally, there are scientific cooperative offices located in four world areas: Montevideo, Cairo, New Delhi and Jakarta.

UNESCO produces numerous and diverse publications—such as Bibliographical Services Throughout the World; Catalogs of Color Reproductions; Study Abroad; Vacations Abroad; The Race Question and Modern Science; and The History of Mankind, Cultural and Scientific Development.

Responsibilities For Non-Self-Governing Territories

The Charter of the United Nations, under Chapter XI, assumes responsibility for and imposes obligations on responsible states in respect to non-self-governing territories. Non-self-governing territories are defined as "territories whose peoples have not yet attained a full measure of self-government" (Article 73). Although this definition appears very broad, in practice, a number of entities which are not states nor clearly independent escape the classification of and provisions pertaining to non-self-governing territories. First, trust territories, because of Charter provisions elsewhere, are exempted from the reporting provision of Chapter XI. Second, overseas territories, that is, noncontiguous entities considered parts of states, are exempted entirely from Chapter XI. The overseas territory of New Caledonia, as part of France, falls in this category. Finally, self-governing entities which are not states, such as Puerto Rico, are also exempted from Chapter XI. An important question arises, however, as to who decides upon these exemptions---the United Nations or individual states? Although the United Nations had repeatedly attempted to make such determinations, in practice, individual states appear to make the final decision. For example, Portugal refused to report under Chapter XI and refused to take her allotted seat on the General Assembly's Committee on Information from Non-Self-Governing Territories, on the grounds that her overseas possessions were an integral part of Portugal. On occasion, the General Assembly has shifted a non-independent territory from the non-self-governing to self-governing classification. This was the case with Puerto Rico, after her commonwealth status was approved in 1952. This determination, in effect, ended United States responsibilities under Chapter XI of the Charter. (Puerto Ricans are United States citizens, subject to the draft, and appeals may be made from Puerto Rican courts to United States courts. Also, the United States is responsible for the defense and foreign affairs of Puerto Rico.) Non-self-governing matters are presently the responsibility of the Committee of Twenty-four, created in 1962 by the Assembly to oversee the application of the Declaration in the Granting of Independence to Colonial Countries and Peoples. The later declaration---along with one contained in the Charter, i.e., the "Declaration Regarding Non-Self-Governing Territories"---establishes the guidelines to be followed by responsible states toward such territories.

States responsible for non-self-governing territories assume certain responsibilities for them by virtue of being members of the United Nations. Such states promise, under Article 73:

to promote . . . the well-being of the inhabitants . . .to ensure . . . political, economic, social and educational advancement . . .[and] . . . to transmit regularly to the

> Secretary General . . . subject to such limitation as
> security and constitutional considerations may require,
> statistical and other information . . . relating to economic,
> social and educational conditions in the territories.

Also, responsible states promise that their policy toward the
territories should take "due account . . . of the interests and
well-being of the rest of the world, in social, economic and
commercial matters" (Article 74). The organs primarily concerned
with the implementation of these provisions are the Special
Committee and the Trusteeship Committee (Fourth) of the General
Assembly. United Nations consideration of non-self-governing
matters revolves, for the most part, around information gathered
from questionnaires completed by the responsible states. Unlike
the questionnaire used by the Trusteeship Council, however, the
completion of the political section is optional. That is, only
the nonpolitical (general information, economic, social, and
educational) sections, because of the provisions of Article 73,
are required. In the past, considerable tension and debate have
developed over the United Nations efforts to implement these
articles. Several colonial powers have held that the above
provisions are only moral obligations, the application of which is
to be determined solely by the responsible states, while many
non-colonial states have viewed the provisions as binding, the
interpretation of which should be determined by the United
Nations.

Part of the UN's concern stems from the Declaration on the
Granting of Independence to Colonial Countries and Peoples,
adopted by the General Assembly on December 14, 1960. Although no
state voted against the Declaration, nine states abstained from
voting--the United States, United Kingdom, Australia, Belgium,
Dominican Republic, France, Portugal, Spain, and South Africa.
The Declaration: (1) views the subjugation of peoples by alien
powers as contrary to the United Nations Charter; (2) gives all
people the right of self-determination in respect to their
political status and their economic, social and cultural
development; (3) calls for an end to any kind of armed action or
repressive measures to prevent dependent people from gaining their
independence; (4) calls for the transference of power without
condition to peoples wishing independence; (5) views an effort to
disrupt the national unity or territorial integrity of a country
as contrary to the Charter of the United Nations; and (6) calls
upon states to observe the United Nations Charter, the Universal
Declaration of Human Rights, and the Declaration on the Granting
of Independence to Colonial Countries and Peoples.

The Trusteeship System

Trust territories are areas under the supervision of an
administering authority in the Trusteeship System. Three types of
areas were originally comtemplated as subject to the status of

trust territories: (1) mandates under the League of Nations; (2) detached territories as the result of World War II; and (3) territories voluntarily placed under the system (such as colonies). The original trust territories were New Guinea, Nauru (Australia); Ruanda-Urundi (Belgium); Cameroons, Togoland (France); Cameroons, Togoland, Tanganyika (United Kingdom); Pacific Islands (United States); Western Samoa (New Zealand); and Somaliland (Italy). All but Somaliland, a former Italian colony detached because of World War II, were League mandates. No additional territories have been voluntarily placed under the system. Presently, only the Pacific Islands remain as trust territories. The rest have become independent or are part of independent states. In the US case, since 1976, the Northern Mariannas have been administered separately from the Marshall Islands and the Caroline Islands. The people of the Northern Marianas approved Commonwealth status and a Constitution in 1975. The US gave formal approval of the constitution in 1977 and the first elections were held in late 1977, with installation in early 1978. The US will end its trust states by December, 1981.

The Trusteeship Council is designated as a principal organ of the United Nations by Article 7 of the United Nations Charter, and it has special responsibilities for the international trusteeship system, provided for by Chapter 12. The objectives of the system, according to Article 76 of the Charter, are:

to further international peace and security; . . . to promote the political, economic, social and educational advancement of the inhabitants of the trust territories, and their progressive development towards self-government or independence as may be appropriate to the particular circumstances of each territory and its people and the freely expressed wishes of the peoples concerned, and as may be provided by the terms of each trusteeship agreement; . . . to encourage respect for human rights and for fundamental freedoms for all without distinction as to race, sex, language, or religion, and to encourage recognition of the interdependence of the peoples of the world; and . . . to insure equal treatment in social, economic, and commercial matters for all members of the United Nations and their nationals and also equal treatment for the latter in the administration of justice, without prejudice to the attainment of the foregoing objectives . . .

The Trusteeship Council

The Trusteeship Council, like the Economic and Social
Council, operates under the authority of the General Assembly
which reviews its work and approves the trusteeship agreements.
The Trusteeship Council has diminished in size as trust
territories have become independent and will disappear entirely
when all such areas have attained their independence.
The Trusteeship Council consists of administering
authorities, permanent members who are also permanent members of
the Security Council, and enough elected members (three-year
terms) so that the Council membership is balanced between trust
and nontrust states. Until 1960 the Council had fourteen members.
Since that time, the size has decreased, as the majority of the
trust territories have become independent or parts of other
independent states. Presently there is one administering member,
the United States, and four nonadministering members, China,
France, United Kingdom, USSR and Australia.
Two sessions of the Council, starting in January and June,
were held each year until 1963. Since then, one session has been
held in May. Special sessions may be held upon the request of the
Security Council, the General Assembly, a majority of members of
the Trusteeship Council, or by a decision of the Trusteeship
Council.
Each member of the Council possesses one vote and decisions
are made by the majority of members present and voting (Article
89). Although the permanent members of the Security Council are
always present on the Council they possess no special voting
privileges.
Trusteeship agreements have specified the terms under which
trust territories were administered by administering authorities.
They were negotiated by the Trusteeship Council with administering
authorities and approved by the Security Council in the case of
strategic trust areas and by the General Assembly for all other
territories.
Article 84 of the Charter provides:
It shall be the duty of the administering authority to ensure
that the trust territory shall play its part in the
maintenance of international peace and security. To this end
the administering authority may make use of volunteer forces,
facilities, and assistance from the trust territory in
carrying out the obligations towards the Security Council
undertaken in this regard by the administering authority, as
well as for local defense and the maintenance of law and
order within the trust territory.
This provision preserved the role of such territories in the
League of Nations system in that mandatories were instructed to
prevent "the establishment of fortifications or military and naval
bases and of military training of the natives for other than

police purposes and the defense of the territory" (Covenant, Article 22, Par. 5). Although the administering authority could not employ conscription it could establish bases and utilize volunteer forces for collective security action as well as local defense and order.

The Administering Authority was the state (or states) responsible, through agreements approved by the General Assembly (or the Security Council in the case of strategic areas), for the development of trust territories in the trusteeship System. The part played by the Administering Authority was an outgrowth of the role of the Mandatory in the League of Nations mandates system. The original Administering Authorities were Australia, Belgium, France, Italy, New Zealand, United Kingdom, and the United States (some with more than one trust territory). All but the United States and Italy had been mandatories in the League system.

Any person has the right to petition the Trusteeship Council regarding conditions in the trust territories with the qualification that petitions should not concern disputes which the courts of the Administering Authority can deal with and should not be directed against court judgments. Court judgments, however, must be based on laws that are consistent with the United Nations Charter and trusteeship agreements. Petitions were sent to the Secretary-General, the Administering Authority, or presented to members of visiting missions dispatched by the Council. The Council considered petitions and made resolutions concerning them to Administering Authorities. Thousands of petitions, covering a wide variety of matters, were received and considered in the operation of the Trusteeship system.

The device of a Standing Committee on Petitions was employed from 1952 to 1962. It was created each session to screen the flow of petitions from the trust territories. The members of the Committee were divided equally between Council members from administering and non-administering states. The Administering Authority concerned had the right to explain and to present views to the Committee, regarding the petitions, prior to the Committee's report to the Council. Since 1962, petition functions have been taken over by the Council itself.

The Council is authorized, by Article 88 of the Charter, to prepare a questionnaire to be completed by the Administering Authority, to be used by the Council in its annual reports. The questionnaire has been complex and probing, covering in detail political, economic, social, education, and security questions as well as other matters. Each report was formally examined by the Council, leading to a general discussion. The usual procedure was to have an opening statement by a representative of the Administering Authority to the Council and then an exchange of written and oral questions and answers between the Authority and members of the Council. Information gathered in this way———along with other data from visiting missions, petitions, and other possible sources, such as the specialized agencies———allowed the

Council to come to conclusions and make recommendations.

The Council made reports to the Security Council for strategic areas and to the General Assembly for all other trust territories. Reports were based on petitions, oral hearings, questionnaires, visiting missions, and other possible sources of information. Reports described conditions, summarized discussions, and listed recommendations for each territory. Possible recommendations to Administering Authorities by the Security Council and the General Assembly were based on these reports. In the case of the General Assembly, the Fourth Committee (Trusteeship) used reports and additional information, such as gathered through oral hearings, to make recommendations to the plenary session of the Assembly.

The Council granted oral hearings upon request, usually in connection with a petition. Such oral hearings were used, for example, in connection with the granting of independence to the Cameroons, Togoland, and Tanganyika.

The Council had the right, under Article 87 of the Charter, to "provide for periodic visits to the respective trust territories at times agreed upon with the administering authority." In practice, each of the territories was visited approximately once every three years, although special missions could be sent at more frequent intervals. The mission normally consisted of four members, two of which are derived from states named by the Administering Authority and two of which come from other states. The information gathered by the mission, on a wide variety of subjects, was be used in the Council's report to the General Assembly and to advise the Administering Authority.

The strategic areas are designated as such in trusteeship agreements. The only trust territories so designated are the Pacific Islands (Marshalls, Carolines, and Marianas, excepting Guam) with the United States as administering authority. These areas were previously Japanese mandates under the League mandates system. The major difference between strategic areas and nonstrategic areas (all others) is that in the case of the former: (1) the Security Council approves (veto applies) the trusteeship agreement; (2) the basic objectives of the trusteeship system are qualified by security considerations; and (3) the Trusteeship Council's supervision powers are less than in the case of nonstrategic areas.

THE INTERNATIONAL COURT OF JUSTICE

The Statute of the Court, after being drafted by the United Nations Committee of Jurists, was accepted at the San Francisco Conference as an integral part of the Charter of the United Nations. There is no way, therefore, for a state to be a member of the United Nations and not be a member of the Court; however, the Statute may be adhered to by states that are not members of the United Nations. The Statute has the same status as any treaty and, therefore, is considered binding. Its seventy Articles provide for the Court's organization, competence, procedures, and amendment procedures to be employed in changing the Statute. Basically, the provisions are similar if not identical to those which created the Permanent Court of International Justice.

Article 7 of the Charter designated the International Court of Justice as one of the Principal organs of the United Nations, while Article 92 defines it as "the principal judicial organ." It operates primarily in the legal sphere. The Court sits in The Hague, Netherlands, in permanent session except during vacation. For the most part, the Court is separated from the mainstream of United Nations politics. Most of the decisions of the Court have touched upon matters of minor consequence. Some non-decisional advisory opinions have, at times, been directed toward crucial or crisis issues. States may, however, without violating international law, ignore the Court's opinions, Whenever the Court is called upon to render decisions. however, states are bound, under Article 94 of the Charter, to adhere to them. It is possible in cases of noncompliance for the Security Council to recommend or decide upon measures "to give effect to the judgment" (Article 94, Par. 2). Under present circumstances, states tend to use the Court only when it is convenient for them to do so.

Amendments to the Statute are made in the same way as amendments to the Charter of the United Nations with the qualification that parties to the Statute who are not members of the United Nations may be permitted to participate in the amendment process under rules established by the General Assembly after a recommendation by the Security Council (Statute, Article 69).

All members of the United Nations are automatically parties to the Statute of the International Court of Justice and therefore members of the Court (Charter, Article 92). A state not a member of the Court may become one upon the recommendation of the Security Council upon conditions established by the General Assembly. For example, Switzerland, San Marino, and Liechtenstein have become members of the Court on the conditions that they accept the provisions of the Statute of the Court and Article 94 of the Charter, requiring compliance with Court decisions, and that they contribute to the expense of the Court.

When the full Court sits, nine judges constitute a quorum.

However, the Court may divide into chambers of three or more judges to deal with certain categories of cases (e.g., labor cases) or form a special chamber for a certain case, if the parties to the case agree. Also, the Court forms annually a chamber of five judges, which, if the parties to a case so desire, hears cases with simplified procedures. Whenever a decision is reached with any of the above arrangements it has the full authority of the Court.

The fifteen judges are elected for nine-year terms (staggered, five judges every three years) by absolute majorities in the Security Council and General Assembly, voting independently of one aother. However, elections are subject to the proviso that no two elected judges be of the same nationality and that the Court, as a whole, be representative of "the main forms of civilization and of the principal legal systems of the world" (Statute, Article 9). If the voting process gives concurrent absolute majorities to more than one national of a single state, only the oldest judge is considered elected. Judges are nominated by national groups used in connection with the Permanent Court of Arbitration. If, however, a state is party to the Statute of the Court but not a member of the Permanent Court, judges are nominated by specially appointed persons in the states concerned. All nominations are to be made from persons "of high moral character, who possess the qualifications required in their respective countries for appointment to the highest judicial office, or are jurisconsults of recognized competence in international law" (Statute, Article 2). National nominating groups are limited to naming four persons, no more than two of whom can be of the nominating group's own nationality. Retiring judges are eligible for reelection.

Should the election process fail to fill all the seats, the elected members of the Court are empowered to do so, within a period fixed by the Security Council. The choice is to be made from those candidates who have already received votes in either the General Assembly or the Security Council. However, a joint conference of representatives of the Security Council and General Assembly (three members from each) should first have attempted to get acceptance by the two organs of candidates selected by the conference.

Permanent members of the Security Council, except China, have been represented on the Court since its existence, but Big Five judges possess no special privileges. If a party to a dispute does not have a judge of its own nationality on the Court, it may choose one for the case even though, presumably, judges are "elected regardless of their nationality." (Compare: Statute, Articles 2 and 3.) While persons are serving as judges they are forbidden from holding any other political, administrative, or professional position.

Sources of Law Applied

When deciding disputes the Court, by provision of Article 38, is allowed to apply: (1) "international conventions, whether general or particular, establishing rules expressly recognized by the contesting states"; (2) "international custom, as evidence of a general practice accepted as law"; (3) "general principles of law recognized by civilized nations," and as "subsidiary means" for the determination of the rules of law; (4) "judicial decisions and the teachings of the most highly qualified publicists" with the proviso that decisions have "no binding force except between the parties and in respect . . . [to a] . . . particular case" (Article 59). The Court can, however, decide a case ex aequo et bono if the parties to the case so agree.

International conventions (treaties) and custom have been treated above under the international law section.

Judicial decisions and teachings of highly qualified publicists are designated by the Statute of the International Court of Justice as "subsidiary means for the determination of the rules of law." Many authors have noted the impact of publicists upon the rules of international custom, related to the fact that judges tend to rely upon the writings of publicists in ascertaining the content of customary law. Basically, then, this Statute provision reaffirms this practice by judges.

The use of judicial decisions to clarify rules, on the other hand, is somewhat obscured by other provisions in the Statute. Article 59 forbids, in effect, the use of the rule 'stare decisis' (considering the decisions of previous cases binding in respect to present cases). However, to the extent that the judges do look to previous cases to clarify rules, it would seem that this activity should shape their decisions in the particular case under consideration.

Use of the Court, Procedures, Opinions, and Judgements

The Court may be used by all members of the United Nations and nonmembers under conditions laid down by the Security Council. The Security Council is forbidden, however, from establishing conditions for nonmembers that would place such states "in a position of inequality before the Court" (Statute, Article 35, Par. 2). The Security Council has required some nonmembers that wish to use the Court to indicate through a declaration to the Registrar of the Court that they will comply with the Statute and rules of the Court in accepting the Court's jurisdiction and be bound by the decisions of the Court. The contribution for Court expenses when nonmembers use the Court is determined by the Court (Article 35, Par. 3).

Decisions of the Court, when legally constituted, are made by a majority of the judges present, with the President or the judge acting (in his absence) casting the deciding vote in case of a tie. It should be noted that this system differs from a simple majority system based upon those present and voting, as used by the General Assembly. Each judge has the right to present a separate opinion concerning a decision of the Court.

The Court has jurisidiction when disputes are referred to it by states (consent of all parties); treaties confer jurisdiction; and parties to a dispute have previously declared themselves bound by the optional clause concerning certain categories of cases. Thus, consent is assumed in all cases prior to the actual exercise of jurisdiction by the Court. However, "in the event of a dispute as to whether the Court has jurisdiction, the matter shall be settled by the decision of the Court" (Article 36, Par. 6). In practice, this right of the Court appears to be partially undercut by the character of reservations adopted by states in accepting the optional clause. If the Court does decide it has jurisdiction, failure to appear by one of the parties cannot prevent an unfavorable judgment. That is, "whenever one of the parties does not appear before the Court, or fails to defend its case, the other party may call upon the Court to decide in favor of its claims" (Statute, Article 53, Par. 1). However, the claim itself, in such a case, must be "well founded in fact and law" (Article 53, Par. 2).

The optional clause, referred to above, is based on Article 36, paragraph 2, of the Statute. It provides that the Court will have jurisdiction in respect to: interpretations of treaties; questions of international law; the existence of facts relating to breaches of international obligations; and the nature and extent of reparations for breaches of international obligations. Jurisdiction is qualified, however, by the stipulation that it applies in cases where the disputing parties indicate, through prior declaration, that they wish the Court to have jurisdiction in such matters "in relation to any other State accepting the same obligation." States, however, may attach reservations to their optional clause declarations. Reservations have been varied and numerous. The United States, for example, exempts from Court jurisdiction: (1) disputes entrusted to other tribunals by prior or future agreement, (2) disputes within the domestic jurisdiction of the United States as determined by the United States; and (3) disputes involving multilateral treaties unless all signatories are parties to the case or the United States agrees to confer jurisdiction. Similar declarations by other states have greatly reduced the significance of Article 36, paragraphs 2 and 6, which indicate that "in the event of a dispute as to whether the Court has jurisdiction, the matter shall be settled by the decision of the Court." The fact that states may make dissimilar declarations and require reciprocity provides a basis for the Court to exclude the application of the optional clause in certain cases on the grounds that both parties have not accepted "the same obligation." Thus, a state, in attempting to press a claim based on the optional clause, may find that its own reservations provide a basis for a counter-claim, which may be accepted by the Court, that the optional clause cannot be applied. Finally, some states have reservations providing for immediate extensions of reservations which, for practical purposes, may allow them to escape an obligation for legal settlement in any dispute.

The Court has the right to call for provisional measures in a case if such measures are necessary to protect the rights of either party. For example, the Court issued such measures in the Anglo-Iranian Oil Company Case (1951), involving the Iranian nationalization of a British oil company, when it called upon the parties to restrain themselves from action that would aggravate the dispute or be harmful to the company (i.e., the prenationalization management was to continue). Such Court measures are binding upon states and, therefore, have the same status as decisions, in contrast to recommendations. In the above case, however, Iran ignored the provisional measures.

Technically, the decisions of the Court are "final and without appeal" (Article 60). However, the Court may continue a case upon the request of any party to the case if a dispute arises as to the meaning and scope of a judgment. Also, a state has a right to ask for a revision if it makes application to the Court within six months of the discovery of a new fact unknown at the time of the case which could have been a decisive factor in the judgment. Such an application cannot be made, however, after ten years of the date of the judgment. The Court, after receiving the application, may open "proceedings for revision" if it agrees that the new fact has the crucial character claimed by the applicant (Article 61, Par. 2).

As is universally the case with courts, the International Court of Justice has no means of its own to enforce its judgments. However, "if any party to a case fails to perform the obligations incumbent upon it under a judgment rendered by the Court, the other party may have recourse to the Security Council, which may, if it deems neseccary, make recommendations or decide upon measures to be taken to give effect to the judgment" (Charter, Article 94, Par. 2). The permanent members of the Security Council, however, stand in a different legal position than other members of the international community on the matter of the enforcement of Court judgments in that they possess the veto power in the application of Article 94, even in their own case. In one case of a clear violation of a Court judgment since World War II, where Albania refused to pay damages in the Corfu Channel case, the injured party, Great Britain, did not appeal to the Security Council. States, individually, of course, may still apply sanctions in cases of failure to adhere to Court judgments if such sanctions are not prohibited by the United Nations Charter.

Court outcomes may be classified as advisory (not binding) and judgements and/or decisions (binding). Advisory opinions may be requested by the Security Council and General Assembly, as authorized by the Charter (Article 96), and by other United Nations organs and specialized agencies if authorized to do so by the General Assembly. The Court normally honors such requests but

has discretion in the matter. Requests, presumably, pertain only
to legal questions. Court procedures during an advisory opinion
are similar to those used in judgments. Generally speaking,
advisory opinions given by the Court have concerned more important
matters than those dealt with in cases leading to judgments.

Advisory opinions are treated first, on a ruling by ruling
basis, followed by cases that have or could have resulted in
judgements (binding decisions).

ADVISORY OPIONIONS FOR THE GENERAL ASSEMBLY

ADVISORY OPINION CONCERNING THE INTERNATIONAL STATUS OF SOUTHWEST
AFRICA

In December, 1949, the General Assembly requested an advisory
opinion from the Court concerning: the status of Southwest
Africa; the obligations of the Union of South Africa in respect to
Southwest Africa; the applicability of certain Charter provisions
in respect to the Union of South Africa's obligations; and the
competence of the Union of South Africa to modify the status of
Southwest Africa. This request stemmed from the refusal of the
Union of South Africa, which acted as a mandatory under the League
in respect to Southwest Africa, to place Southwest Africa under
the trusteeship system of the United Nations at the end of World
War II. With the founding of the United Nations, all other League
mandatories had placed their mandates under the United Nations
trusteeship system making them trust territories. The crucial
question in this case concerned whether or not mandate
responsibilities continued for the Union of South Africa in spite
of the fact that the League and the League machinery concerning
mandates had been dissolved. The Court replied, on January 11,
1950, that the Union of South Africa's responsibilities continue
under the United Nations, but that the United Nations supervision
is limited to the kind of supervision exercised by the League.
Further, although the Union of South Africa was not required to
place Southwest Africa into the trusteeship system, nevertheless,
the Court advised, Southwest Africa's status as a mandate could
not be altered unilaterally by the Union of South Africa.

ADVISORY OPINION CONCERNING THE INTERPRETATION OF PEACE TREATIES
WITH BULGARIA, HUNGARY, AND ROMANIA

In October, 1949, the General Assembly requested that the
Court give an advisory opinion concerning the responsibilities of
the signatories of certain peace treaties concluded in Paris in
1947, and the rights of the Secretary-General of the United
Nations in respect to these peace treaties. Under the treaties,

Bulgaria, Hungary, and Romania agreed to allow human rights and fundamental freedoms to every person under their jurisdiction. In case of disputes concerning the conduct of the parties, arbitral commissions were to be composed. The third member of such commissions was to be appointed by the Secretary-General in case of disagreement between the parties concerning the third member. Although the allied powers claimed that a dispute did exist over the provisions to the treaties, Bulgaria, Hungary, and Romania refused to help constitute any commissions. In view of these events, the General Assembly asked the Court: whether a dispute did in fact exist between the signatories; whether the three states concerned had an obligation to appoint representatives to a commission, and should they fail to do so whether the Secretary-General would have the right to appoint a member; and whether the member appointed by the Secretary-General, in addition to one appointed by the allies, would constitute a competent commission able to make decisions in respect to the matters in dispute. The Court advised, on March 30, 1950, that a dispute did exist and that signatories were obligated to appoint their respective representatives to a commission. On July 18, 1950, however, the Court advised that the Secretary-General's appointment of a third member was contingent upon the prior appointment of the other commission members. Because the question of the competence of a two-member commission was contingent upon the right of the Secretary-General to appoint one member, the Court did not direct itself to this question.

ADVISORY OPINION IN RESPECT TO CERTAIN EXPENSES OF THE UNITED NATIONS

On December 20, 1961, the General Assembly requested an advisory opinion from the Court concerning the propriety of treating special assessments for peace-keeping operations as expenses of the organization to be "borne by the members as apportioned by the General Assembly" (Article 17, Par. 2). This request was precipitated by the failure of several states to pay their special assessments in respect to the peace-keeping operations related to the Suez and Congo crises. The Court advised on July 20, 1962, that such expenditures properly constituted expenses of the United Nations and, therefore, should be borne by the members as apportioned by the General Assembly. The advice, however, had little effect upon the major delinquents---namely, the USSR, France, Belgium, South Africa, Portugal, and several Arab states.

ADVISORY OPINION IN RESPECT TO REPARATIONS FOR INJURIES SUFFERED IN THE SERVICE OF THE UNITED NATIONS

In December, 1948, the General Assembly requested an advisory opinion from the Court concerning the right of the United Nations to bring a claim against a government responsible for injury to a United Nations agent in order to obtain reparations for the United Nations, the agent, or persons related to him. Also, the General Assembly wished to know whether such claims are reconcilable with possible claims possessed by the state of the injured agent. The Court advised, on April 11, 1949, that the United Nations has a right to bring claims on its own behalf for its injured agents and on behalf of persons entitled to compensation due to their relationship with the injured agent. Such claims were not to be viewed as incompatible, in principle, with the claims of the state of the victim, and various legal contingencies could be provided for through international agreements. The advisory opinion was precipitated by the assassination of Count Faulk Bernadotte, in Palestine, while serving as a United Nations mediator.

ADVISORY OPINION IN RESPECT TO RESERVATIONS TO THE GENOCIDE CONVENTION

In November, 1950, the General Assembly requested an advisory opinion from the Court concerning the legal consequences of reservations made in adhering to the Genocide Convention. Specifically, the General Assembly wished to know the consequences of possible objections to reservations in respect to the legal obligations between all parties in cases where: states had ratified the Convention; states were signatories but had not ratified the Convention; and states could exercise the right of becoming a signatory but had not done so. THese questions were precipitated by the fact that although the Genocide Convention makes no provisions for reservations, nevertheless, a number of states had made reservations in ratifying the convention. The Court ruled on May 28, 1951, that the legal effect of reservations was not to automatically eliminate a state as a party to the Convention, but, rather, was dependent upon the compatibility of each reservation with the purpose of the Convention. In the case of an objection, the state making the objection must judge whether or not the reservations of the reserving state are incompatible with the purpose of the Conveniton. If it judges that they are, from its prespective, the reserving state is not a member of the Convention. On the other hand, if the reservations are considered compatible, the reserving state may be considered a party to the Convention. In the case of states which are signatories, but which have not ratified, or which are entitled to sign, but have not signed, such advice becomes applicable only after ratification.

ADVISORY OPINION IN RESPECT TO THE ADMISSIBILITY OF HEARINGS BY
THE COMMITTEE ON SOUTHWEST AFRICA

In December, 1955, the General Assembly requested an advisory
opinion from the Court concerning the compatibility of the
practice of allowing the Committee on Southwest Africa the right
to grant hearings to petitioners concerning Southwest Africa with
the Court's earlier advisory opinion of July, 1950, concerning
Southwest Africa. It was the contention of the Union of South
Africa that the practice of granting oral hearings exceeded the
authority of the General Assembly. The Court ruled on June 1,
1956, that the General Assembly's practices were consistent with
its previous advisory opinion.

ADVISORY OPINION IN RESPECT TO THE COMPETENCE OF THE GENERAL
ASSEMBLY REGARDING ADMISSION TO THE UNITED NATIONS

In November, 1949, the General Assembly requested an advisory
opinion from the Court concerning the right of the General
Assembly to admit a state on its own into the United Nations in
the absence of a recommendation on the part of the Security
Council. This request was precipitated by the continuing deadlock
and continued use of the veto power in the Security Council in
respect to a large number of applicant states. The Court replied
on March 3, 1950, that the Charter requires an affirmative
recommendation of the Security Council prior to a decision of the
General Assembly to admit a state (Article 4, Par. 2).

ADVISORY OPINION IN RESPECT TO THE CONDITIONS OF ADMISSION OF A
STATE TO MEMBERSHIP IN THE UNITED NATIONS

In November, 1948, the General Assembly adopted a resolution
requesting an advisory opinion concerning the condition under
which a state could be admitted to the United Nations.
Specifically, the General Assembly wished to know whether members
voting on membership could make their vote contingent upon
conditions not specified in the United Nations Charter and,
particularly, a condition that an affirmative vote for one state
be linked to affirmative vote for another. This request related
to the failure of a number of states to gain admission to the
United Nations because members of the Security Council made their
votes contingent upon certain conditions of the kind indicated
above. The Court replied on May 28, 1948. It maintained that the
only proper conditions for admission were those found in the

Charter. That is, a state applying for membership should be
"peace-loving" and be "able and willing" to carry out Charter
obligations (Article 4).

ADVISORY OPINION IN RESPECT TO THE EFFECT OF AWARDS OF COMPENSATION MADE BY THE UNITED NATIONS ADMINISTRATIVE COUNCIL

During its Eighth Session, the General Assembly requested an
advisory opinion from the Court concerning the right of the
General Assembly to refuse to give effect to certain decisions of
the United Nations Administrative Tribunal. The Tribunal had been
created by the Assembly in 1949 to hear cases relating to the
employment of members of the Secretariat. The advisory opinion
was precipitated by certain awards made by the Tribunal in
connection with members of the Secretariat who had been dismissed
by the Secretary-General after their refusal to testify before a
US Congressional committee in connection with possible subversive
activities. Specifically, the General Assembly wished to know the
grounds upon which it could refuse to compensate the individuals
concerned in accordance with the Tribunal's decision. The Court
ruled on July 13, 1954, that, as a judicial body, the Tribunal's
decisions were final and could not be overruled by the General
Assembly.

ADVISORY OPINION IN RESPECT TO VOTING PROCEDURE ON QUESTIONS RELATING TO REPORTS AND PETITIONS CONCERNING THE TERRITORY OF SOUTHWEST AFRICA

In November, 1954, the General Assembly requested an advisory
opinion from the Court concerning the propriety voting procedures
used in connection with reports and petitions concerning Southwest
Africa. The General Assembly had adopted a rule whereby voting on
matters concerning Southwest Africa would require a two-thirds
majority. It was the contention of the Union of South Africa that
the General Assembly's decision concerning voting exceeded its
supervisory powers. The Court advised on June 7, 1955, that the
voting rule of the General Assembly was not inconsistent with the
guidelines of its previous advisory opinion. To impose a unanimity
system upon the General Assembly in respect to such matters would
be inconsistent with Charter provisions concerning the Assembly's
voting procedures.

ADVISORY OPINION IN RESPECT TO THE SPANISH SAHARA

In 1976 the former Spanish Sahara was partitioned and annexed
to the neighboring states of Morocco and Mauritania. The native
Polisario Front fought both countries in order to be independent
as the Saharan Arab Democratic Republic. Neither the OAU nor the
UN were able to obtain a settlement.
In 1975, the General Assembly requested an advisory opinion
from the Court concerning the question of colonialism in the
Spanish Sahara. On December 13, 1975 the Court ruled that
Algeria, Mauritania and Morocco were not linked to Spain in such a
way that there was a conflict with the General Assembly resolution
on decolonization. (A Chronology and Fact Book of the UN,
Chamberlin, Hovet and Hovet. 1976. N.Y. R341.23 p. 132)

ADVISORY OPINION FOR THE GENERAL ASSEMBLY'S ADMINISTRATIVE AND
BUDGETARY COMMITTEE

ADVISORY OPINION IN RESPECT TO JUDGEMENT NO. 158 OF THE UN
ADMINISTRATIVE TRIBUNAL

The General Assembly's Administrative and Budgetary Committee
made application for review of Judgement no. 158 of the UN
Administrative Tribunal in 1975. The Tribunal had ruled that all
South African employees of the UN would be terminated by the end
of the fiscal year. The Court ruled that no international civil
servant could be terminated without just cause (criminal
negligence, criminal acts, or incapacitation). The employees were
never terminated.

ADVISORY OPINION FOR THE INTER-GOVERNMENTAL MARITIME CONSULTATIVE
ORGANIZATION

ADVISORY OPINION IN RESPECT TO THE CONSTITUTION OF THE MARITIME
SAFETY OF THE INTER-GOVERNMENTAL MARITIME CONSULTATIVE
ORGANIZATION

The Assembly of the Inter-Governmental Maritime Consultative
Organization (IMCO) requested an advisory opinion from the Court
after a dispute arose in connection with the Assembly's election
of the Maritime Safety Committee. According to the constitution

of IMCO, eight of the fourteen members of the Maritime Safety
Committee should be the largest ship-owning nations. These were
designated by the Assembly as France, Federal Republic of Germany,
Italy, Japan, Netherlands, Norway, United Kingdom, and the United
States. These states were elected to the Maritime Safety
Committee by the Assembly. Liberia and Panama, however, have more
registered gross tonnage than some of those states designated as
the largest ship-owning nations. A dispute arose as to whether
registration should be the defining criterion of a ship-owning
nation. That is, it was the contention of Liberia and Panama, in
view of their amount of registered tonnage, that they should be
included among the eight states elected to the Maritime Safety
Committee as the largest ship-owning nations. Other states
maintain that registration was not an adequate criterion,
especially because both complaining states allow foreign
registration, which does not create a genuine connection between
them and the ships in question. The Court ruled on January 8,
1960, that registration was a proper criterion in identifying the
largest ship-owning nations, and, therefore, the Maritime Safety
Committee was improperly constituted in terms of its constitution.

ADVISORY OPINION FOR THE UNITED NATIONS ECONOMIC AND SOCIAL
COUNCIL

ADVISORY OPINION IN RESPECT TO THE JUDGMENTS OF THE ADMINISTRATIVE
TRIBUNAL OF THE INTERNATIONAL LABOR ORGANIZATION COMPLAINTS MADE
AGAINST UNESCO

In November, 1955, UNESCO challenged certain decisions made
by the Administrative Tribunal of the International Labor
Organization and requested an advisory opinion from the Court.
Arrangements had been made for UNESCO to use the ILO Tribunal in
certain cases concerning the employment rights of UNESCO's staff.
The request was precipitated by a favorable judgment by the
Tribunal for certain UNESCO staff members. Questions were raised,
however, as to whether this type of case properly fell under the
jurisdiction of the Tribunal. The dispute centered on the right
of the Director-General to refuse to renew contracts that had been
held on a fixed-term basis in light of previously announced
administrative procedures. UNESCO was also interested in having
an opinion from the Court concerning the propriety of the
Director-General's actions, in terms of the good of the service,
and the propriety of certain Tribunal announcements. The Court
advised on October 23, 1956, that the Tribunal was within its
jurisdiction to hear the case in question. Since the statute of
the Tribunal permitted the International Court of Justice to make
advisory opinions in respect to jurisdiction, but not in regard to

judgments, the Court would not advise on other points. The Court advised, however, that because the Tribunal was properly exercising its jurisdiction, it decisions should be considered valid and binding.

ADVISORY OPINION FOR THE SECURITY COUNCIL

ADVISORY OPINION IN RESPECT TO THE CONTINUED PRESENCE OF SOUTH AFRICA IN NAMIBIA (SOUTHWEST AFRICA)

In 1970 Namibia initiated proceedings against South Africa and in June, 1971, the Court ruled that South Africa was occupying Namibia illegally and called for South Africa to withdraw from Namibia immediately. In addition, the Court asked the member states of the UNited Nations to refrain from dealing with South Africa in any way that might imply legal recognition or support for that nation, and stated that it was incumbent upon non-United Nations members to support the Court's position. The United States accepted the ruling fully, whereas the United Kingdom and France declared that they were unable to support the Court fully. In May, 1971, the Court had rejected as irrelevant South African proposals to conduct a plebiscite in South Africa. This advisory opinion has been rejected by South Africa. In 1978 the Security Council approved the western plan for the independence of Namibia. The plan had also been endorsed by SWAPO, the guerrilla group fighting for the independence of Namibia. Essentially, the plan called for: (1) UN troops to oversee the ceasefire and departure of South African troops; (2) UN supervision of elections to be held; and (3) the re-uniting of Walvis Bay with Namibia. The Security Council also determined the size and composition of the military forces to implement the plan. South Africa has rejected this plan for Namibia and planned to hold its own election within Namibia by the end of 1978, prior to the proposed UN-sponsored elections.

AERIAL INCIDENT OF OCTOBER 7, 1952 (UNITED STATES VS. USSR)

The United States instituted proceedings before the Court on June 2, 1952, concerning actions of an aircraft of the USSR against a United States military aircraft off Japan on October 7, 1952. The USSR refused to accept the jurisdiction of the Court and held the United States responsible for the incident. In view of this, the Court ended consideration of the matter in March, 1956.

AERIAL INCIDENT OF MARCH 10. 1953 (UNITED STATES vs. CZECHOSLOVAKIA)

The United States instituted proceedings before the Court against Czechoslovakia in March 9, 1955, concerning the behavior of Czechoslovakian aircraft on March 10, 1953, within the US zone of occupation in Germany. Czechoslovakia denied any responsibility and refused to be a party to the case. In view of this, the Court ended consideration of the matter on March 14, 1956.

AERIAL INCIDENT OF SEPTEMBER 4, 1954 (UNITED STATES vs. THE USSR)

The United States instituted proceedings on August 22, 1958, before the Court against the USSR concerning the behavior of the latter's military aircraft over the Sea of Japan against a military aircraft of the US Navy. The USSR denied responsibility for the incident and refused to give the Court jurisdiction. In view of this, the Court ended its consideration of the case in December, 1958.

AERIAL INCIDENT OF NOVEMBER 7, 1954 (UNITED STATES vs. THE USSR)

The United States instituted proceedings on July 7, 1959, against the Soviet Union concerning the destruction of a United States military craft over Hokkaido, Japan, in November, 1954. The USSR denied responsibility in the case and refused to view the question as open to judicial settlement. In view of these facts, the Court ended its consideration of the case on October 7, 1959.

AERIAL INCIDENT OF JULY 27, 1955 (ISRAEL vs. BULGARIA)

Israel instituted proceedings before the Court, in October of 1957, against Bulgaria concerning an aerial incident on July 27, 1955, involving Bulgarian anti-aircraft fire against an Israel airline. Israel claimed that Bulgaria was bound to submit the dispute to the Court's jurisdiction on the grounds that the Bulgarian adherence to the optional clause in 1921 became effective upon Bulgaria's admission to the United Nations in 1955. Bulgaria claimed that she was no longer bound under the provisions of compulsory jurisdiction due to the dissolution of the Permanent Court of International Justice. Although Article 36, paragraph 5,

of the Statute of the International Court of JUstice continues
obligations in respect to the optional clause assumed under the
old Court, the Court ruled in May, 1959, that these provisions
pertained only to original members, that is, signatories of the
Charter, and not to subsequent members. Therefore, the Court was
without jurisdiction in this particular case.

AMBATIELOS CASE

On April 9, 1951, Greece instituted proceedings with the
Court on behalf of a Greek national, Ambatielos, who claimed
damages due to a failure of the United Kingdom to fulfill
contractual terms made in 1919 concerning the purchase of
steamships. Greece maintained that certain treaties concluded in
1886 and 1926 between Greece and the United Kingdom created an
obligation on the part of the United Kingdom to arbitrate the
dispute. The United Kingdom maintained that the International
Court of Justice possessed no jurisdiction in the case. On July
1, 1952, the Court ruled that it possessed jurisdiction to decide
whether the United Kingdom had a duty to arbitrate but lacked
jurisdiction to decide upon the merits of the case. The Court
ruled on May 19, 1953, that the treaties in question did obligate
the United Kingdom to cooperate with Greece in constituting a
Commission of Arbitration.

ANGLO-IRANIAN OIL COMPANY CASE

The United Kingdom instituted proceedings before the Court on
May 26, 1951, in connection with the responsibilities of Iran
relating to the latter's nationalization on May 1, 1951, of the
Anglo-Iranian Oil Company. The United Kingdom claimed that Iran
was obligated to arbitrate the dispute because of an agreement
between Iran and the company in 1933 and because Iran had accepted
the optional clause, providing for compulsory jurisdiction, under
the Statute of the Permanent Court of International Justice. In
view of the fact that Iran was continuing with the
nationalization, the United Kingdom requested in June that the
Court issue provisional measures to preserve the rights of the
company. Such provisional measures were issued by the Court in
July and both parties were requested not to take action that would
hinder the company or further aggravate the dispute. Iran,
however, ignored this order and maintained that the Court did not
possess jurisdiction in the case. On July 22, 1952, the Court
declared that it was without jurisdiction on the dispute because
the Iranian adherence to the optional clause only pertained to
treaties ratified after her adherence, and that the contract

between Iran and the Company did not constitute an international treaty. At the time the judgment was given, the provisional measures of July, 1951, were revoked.

ANTARCTICA CASES

The United Kingdom instituted proceedings before the Court on May 4, 1955, against Chile and Argentina in respect to certain disputed claims of title in Antarctica. Neither Chile nor Argentina would accept the jurisdiction of the Court and, therefore, the Court ended consideration of the matter.

THE ASYLUM CASE

Columbia and Peru instituted proceedings before the Court on February 1, 1949.

On January 3, 1949, a Peruvian national, Haya da la Torre, accused by the Peruvian Government of instigating a rebellion, was given asylum by the Columbian Embassy in Lima. The Colombian Government asked the Peruvian Government to give safe conduct to the refugee so that he could leave the country. The dispute over the matter led to applications to the Court by both concerning a number of legal matters. The basic question was whether the behavior of the parties was consistent with treaties between them, in particular, the Pan-American Havana Convention on Asylum, of 1928. The Court ruled in November, 1950, that the Colombian Embassy had improperly granted asylum in terms of the Havana Convention, because of a time difference (too long) between the commission of the offense and the time when asylum was sought and, further, that Colombia had no right, in terms of the treaty, to determine unilaterally the nature of an offense for which asylum could be granted. The treaty allowed asylum for political offenses but not for criminal offenses, although such a determination could not be made unilaterally by the state offering asylum. However, in respect to this last point, the Court also pointed out that Peru had not demonstrated that the fugitive properly belonged in the criminal class. Finally, in view of the circumstances and these decisions, Peru was not bound to guarantee safe passage. A request by Colombia on the same day of the judgment as to whether it was bound to surrender Haya de la Torre to Peru was dismissed by the Court on the grounds that new questions were being raised which would require a new case.

CORFU CHANNEL CASE

The United Kingdom and Albania instituted proceedings before the Court on April 10, 1947.

The Curfu Channel case arose after two British warships struck mines in October, 1946, in the Corfu Channel, which constitutes part of the Albanian territorial waters. The United Kingdom presented the case to the Security Council in January, 1947, after sweeping the Channel of mines in order to acquire evidence. After three months of consideration, the Security Council recommended that the parties refer the dispute to the International Court of Justice. An Albanian objection that the Court did not have jurisdiction was rejected on March 25, 1948. In view of this, the two parties agreed to submit the following questions to the Court: Is Albania responsible under international law for the explosions which occured on October 22, 1946, in Albanian waters and for the damage and loss of human life? Is there any duty to pay compensation? Has the United Kingdom violated the sovereignty of Albania by reason of the acts of the Royal Navy in Albanian waters on October 22 and on November 12-13, 1946? Is there any duty for the United Kingdom to give satisfaction to Albania?

The Court ruled on April, 1949, that the mines could not have been laid without the knowledge of the Albanian Government and, therefore, Albania was responsible. The Court did not determine, however, whether Albania had laid the mines. Because Albania was ruled responsible, the Court assessed a reparation on December 15, 1949. of $2,400,000 to be paid by Albania to the United Kingdom.

The Court held that the initial passage on October 22 was an innocent one and, therefore, proper under international law applying to straits. However, the later mine-sweeping activities in November were a violation of Albanian sovereignty. In spite of this, the United Kingdom was not required to give satisfaction to Albania because the Court declaration, itself, constitutes adequate satisfaction.

Albania refused to pay the assessed reparations.

CASE CONCERNING THE APPLICATION OF THE CONVENTION OF 1902 GOVERNING THE GUARDIANSHIP OF INFANTS

On November 28, 1958, the Netherlands instituted proceedings before the Court about the applicability of the Hague Convention of 1902, concerning an infant of Netherlands nationality. The Netherlands claimed that the national law of the infant sould be applicable in this case rather than Swedish law, in terms of the requirements of the Convention, and initiated the case to obtain guardianship of the child who was Dutch born but residing in Sweden. The child's mother, a Swedish national, died and the child was living with her father, a Netherlands national. The court ruled against the Netherlands and found that since the infant resided in Sweden, she was bound by Swedish law as the Convention of 1902 did not exclude a foreigner residing in another country from obeying the local laws of her residence.

CASE CONCERNING THE ARBITRAL AWARD MADE BY THE KING OF SPAIN ON DECEMBER 23, 1906

On July 1, 1958, Honduras and Nicaragua, after a prior agreement to do so, submitted an application to the Court concerning a boundary dispute between them. This dispute related to certain boundary decisions by the King of Spain, in 1906, concerning portions of their mutual frontiers. The king's arbitration powers in the case were based upon a convention signed by the two states in October, 1894, which after drawing boundary lines left disputed points unsettled by other means up to the determination of the Government of Spain. Nicaragua had never been satisfied with the 1906 decisions and the resulting dispute led to the application before the Court. In November, 1960, the Court ruled that the procedures concerning the award of 1906 were valid and, therefore, the 1906 award was binding upon Nicaragua.

CASE CONCERNING THE BARCELONA TRACTION, LIGHT AND POWER CO. LTD. (1958)

Belgium filed an application before the Court on September 23, 1958, against Spain concerning some 1948 bankruptcy proceedings in Spain involving the Barcelona Traction, Light and Power Company, Limited. Because the company in question was owned primarily by Belgium nationals and Belgium considered the Spanish actions to be illegal under international law, Belgium asked that the Company's rights be restored and compensation be given. Negotiations between the parties, however, led the Belgian Government to inform the Court that it was terminating proceedings, and after this was consented to by the Spanish Government the Court ended its consideration of the case in April, 1961.

CASE CONCERNING THE BARCELONA TRACTION, LIGHT AND POWER CO.,LTD. (1962)

On June 19, 1962, Belgium instituted proceedings before the Court against Spain concerning the Spanish responsibilities regarding the Barcelona Traction, Light, and Power Company,

Limited. Previously, Belgium had instituted proceedings in 1958, on the same subject, but had ended proceedings when it appeared that the negotiations would lead to a settlement of the dispute. Under the new application, the Court was asked to determine that Spain had acted illegally under international law and to set the amount of compensation due Belgium. Consideration of the case began in 1964, and the case was decided on February 5, 1970, with the Court rejecting the Belgian claim.

CASE CONCERNING THE COMPAGNIE DU PORT, DES QUAIS ET DES ENTREPOTS DE BEYROUTH AND THE SOCIETE RADIO-ORIENT

On February 13, 1959, France instituted proceedings before the Court against Lebanon. The disagreement centered on Lebanese measures against two French companies which France felt to be incompatible with certain agreements concluded in 1948 between the two nations. The Court ended its consideration of the matter on August 31, 1960, after satisfactory arrangements had been worked out between the parties.

CASE CONCERNING THE NORTHERN CAMEROONS

The Republic of Cameroon instituted proceedings before the Court on May 30, 1961, against the United Kingdom, concerning the incorporation of Northern Cameroons as a part of Nigeria instead of the Republic of Cameroon. According to the Republic of Cameroon such incorporation was in violation of the Trusteeship Agreement established under the United Nations. In view of the fact that the General Assembly had terminated the Trusteeship agreement and had provided for the incorporation, the Court refused to adjudicate the case on the grounds that any possible Court decision, in terms of the situation, would be without consequence.

CASE CONCERNING THE PROTECTION OF FRENCH NATIONALS AND PROTECTED PERSONS IN EGYPT

A case initiated by France against Egypt concerning the legality of Egyptian measures against the persons and property of French nationals within Egypt was dropped from Court consideration in March, 1951, by agreement of the parties when Egyptian practice was altered to suit France.

CASE CONCERNING RIGHTS OF NATIONALS OF THE THE UNITED STATES IN
MOROCCO

On October 28, 1950, France applied to the Court in
connection with a dispute with the United States over the rights
of American nationals in Morocco relating to treaties between the
United States and Morocco dating back to 1836. The issue had been
precipitated by a French attempt to apply licensing controls on
certain imports through a decree issued in 1948. Other issues
included the extent and application of US consular jurisdiction
and a US claim that US consent was necessary before laws and
regulations could be applied to US nationals in the French zone of
Morocco. Also, the United States claimed immunity for US
nationals concerning certain taxes and a system of validation of
imports used in connection with customs and assessments. The
Court ruled on August 27, 1952, that the decree imposing import
controls was inconsistent with the treaty responsibilities of
Morocco; the United States could properly exercise jurisdiction
through the consular courts in respect to civil and criminal cases
involving US citizens; the United States could not claim
jurisdiction in such cases when the only defendant was a US
national or under US protection; and US nationals possess no
immunity from taxes unless immunity has been specified in a
treaty.

CASES CONCERNING SOUTHWEST AFRICA

On November 4, 1960, both Ethiopia and Liberia instituted
proceedings before the Court against South Africa concerning the
obligation of South Africa in respect to Southwest Africa. The
Court was asked to declare that Southwest Africa remained a
mandate, and that South Africa had violated its obligation as a
mandatory by failing to promote the well-being of the inhabitants
in Southwest Africa because of the practice of apartheid. The
Court ruled against South Africa's preliminary objections
concerning the Court's jurisdiction on December 21, 1962, and
proceeded to consider the merits of the case. In spite of this
ruling, however, the Court on July 1, 1966, dismissed the
complaints of Ethiopia and Liberia on the technical grounds that
they lacked sufficient legal interest in the case. In its ruling
the Court relied upon a standing doctrine which requires that
states using the Court have a direct, personal interest in the
outcome. An unusual feature of the case relates to the fact that
the President of the Court used his power to break a tie vote for
the first time since before World War II. The fact that this case
relates to the emotional topic of apartheid, along with the other
features indicated above, makes it the most controversial one in

the history of the Court.

CASE CONCERNING SOVEREIGNTY OVER CERTAIN FRONTIER LAND

Belgium and the Netherlands asked the Court in March, 1957, to settle a dispute between them concerning plots of land on their mutual frontier. Netherlands based its case upon certain agreements made in 1836 and 1841; on the other hand, Belgium relied primarily upon determinations found in a Boundary Convention of 1843. It was Netherlands' cntention that the latter agreement, although giving possession of the plots in question to Belgium, was in error in that, presumably, the determinations made should have been compatible with the earlier agreements. Also Netherlands maintained that actual sovereignty over the plots in question had been wielded by the Netherlands, rather than Belgium, since the 1843 agreements. The Court ruled on June 20, 1959, that the 1843 agreement was valid and without error and that the Netherlands claims concerning the exercise of sovereignty were basically unfounded. Therefore, the Court awarded to plots in question to Belgium.

CASE CONCERNING THE TEMPLE OF PREAH VIHEAR

Cambodia instituted proceedings before the Court on October 6, 1959, concerning Thailand's occupation of the Temple of Preah Vihear, a temple in ruins but of considerable religious significance for Cambodians. In its application Cambodia asked for a determination to establish her sovereign rights in respect to the temple area and, also, to have Thailand remove her armed forces from Cambodian soil. After dispensing with Thailand's preliminary objections concerning the Court's jurisdiction, the Court ruled on June 15, 1962, that Thailand cannot properly occupy the Temple in view of the fact that it is located in Cambodian territory. In addition, the Court ruled that Thailand has an obligation to replace artifacts removed from the Temple during its occupation.

ELECTRICITE DE BEYROUTH CO. CASE

On August 11, 1953, France instituted proceedings before the Court against Lebanon concerning the compatibility of Lebanese actions in respect to a French company, the Electricite de Beyrouth Co., located in Lebanon, and certain agreements between Lebanon and France concluded in 1948. The Court ended

consideration of the matter on July 29, 1954, after the Lebanese
Government entered into arrangements with the company that were
agreeable to France.

FISHERIES CASE

In 1935, a Norwegian decree restricted certain fishing
grounds off the coast of Norway to Norwegian fishermen and drew
the boundaries, for the area concerned, by following lines
established in terms of the furthermost headland points on an
irregular coast. The United Kingdom applied to the Court, on
September 8, 1949, asking it to decide whether the Norwegian
procedures utilized were legal and whether damages were due to
Britain because of the Norwegian exclusion of British ships from
an area which Britain viewed as part of the high seas. The Court
upheld the Norwegian position, on December 18, 1951, by deciding
that neither Norwegian fishing zones nor the methods of
determining the fishing zones were contrary to international law.
In view of these decisions, the United Kingdom had no basis upon
which to claim damages.

FISHERIES JURISDICTION CASES

West Germany and the United Kingdom instituted proceedings
against Iceland on March 2, 1972.
In 1972, two orders were issued, which constituted interim
measures of protection for the United Kingdom and the Federal
Republic of Germany. The orders stated that Iceland must not
interfere with British and West German trawlers, outside a 12-mile
territorial limit, pending a final judgment on a proposed 50-mile
limit. Requested by the British government, these orders were
refused by Iceland, which did not admit Court jurisdiction.

HAYA DE LA TORRE CASE

Although technically a separate case, in fact, the Haya de la
Torre case grew out of the Colombian Embassy asylum case. When
the Court, in the latter case, refused to give an interpretation
specifying Colombia's responsibilities in respect to surrendering
the refugee, Haya de la Torre, Colombia made a new application to
the Court. In view of the Court's previous decision, Peru called
upon Colombia to turn over Haya de la Torre and to terminate the
asylum. Colombia maintained, however, that neither her treaty
obligations nor the decision in the Colombian Embassy asylum case

dictated this course of action. The Court, basically, upheld the
Colombian point of view in rendering its judgment in June, 1951.
The Court declared that, although Peru had a legal right to demand
termination of asylum because it had been irregularly granted,
nevertheless, Colombia was not legally bound to turn Haya de la
Torre over to Peru. The Havana Convention, upon which the case
partially rested, required the surrender of common criminals but
not political offenders. The matter was finally settled through
bilateral negotiations between Colombia and Peru.

INTERHANDEL CASE

On October 1, 1957, Switzerland instituted proceedings before
the Court against the United States concerning the US take-over of
the shares of the General Aniline and Film Corporation in 1942.
The United States justified its behavior on the grounds that
although Interhandel, the company owning the shares, was
registered in Switzerland, it was controlled and/or owned by I. G.
Farbenindustrie which, in 1942, was an "enemy" firm. The Swiss
Government, in its application, asked that the Court either rule
on the merits of the case or judge that the United States had
responsibility in terms of an existing treaty to submit the
dispute to conciliation, arbitration, or judicial settlement.
The Swiss Government then called for Court provisional measures to
prevent the sale of the assets in question. The Court in October,
1957, denied the need for provisional measures on the grounds that
judicial proceedings within the United States would prevent the
sale of the assets for a considerable length of time and that the
United States had stated that it did not intend to sell the assets
in view of the circumstances. On March 21, 1959, the Court ruled
against the Swiss application on the grounds that the company in
question had failed to exhaust local remedies available to it in
the circumstances. Later the Court determined that it lacked
jurisdiction, in view of the United States' terms of acceptance of
the optional clause which prevented Court jurisdiction in those
cases where the question was one of domestic jurisdiction as
determined by the United States.

MINQUIERS AND ECREHOS CASE

France and the United Kingdom through a special agreement
requested on December 14, 1951, that the Court determine title in
respect to the Minquiers and Ecrehos island groups situated in the
English Channel. The British and French claims were based on
certain medieval treaties and historical facts surrounding the
conquest of England by the Duke of Normandy in 1066 and subsequent

events. The Court decided on November 17, 1953, in favor of the
United Kingdom, stressing evidences of actual control.

CASE OF THE MONETARY GOLD REMOVED FROM ROME IN 1943

Italy instituted proceedings before the Court against France,
the United Kingdom, and the United States on May 19, 1953,
concerning gold taken from Germany as the result of World War II.
The three states in question had formed a commission to allocate
such gold on the basis of a 1946 agreement concerning reparations.
The United Kingdom made a claim upon the gold, originally
Albanian, to compensate her in regard to a Court judgment in 1946
concerning the Corfu Channel incident. Italy claimed the gold on
the grounds that she had suffered damages from an Albanian law
nationalizing the Albanian State Bank, which was owned primarily
by the Italian state. Albania claimed the gold on the grounds
that it was the property of the Albanian State Bank. The Court
ruled on June 15, 1954, that it lacked jurisdiction in the matter
because such a case required consent which had not been given.
For this reason, the Court could not decide between the claims of
Italy and Albania on the one hand or Italy and the United Kingdom
on the other.

NORTH SEA CONTINENTAL SHELF CASE

On February 20, 1969, the Court gave a judgment concerning a
dispute submitted on February 20, 1967, by the Netherlands,
Denmark, and the Federal Republic of Germany, concerning the
delimitation of the North Sea Continental Shelf. Denmark and the
Netherlands contended that the Federal Republic of Germany had
violated its continental boundaries. The case was of special
importance because of the presumed presence of natural gas and oil
deposits under the bed of the North Sea.
The Court was asked to state the principles and rules of
international law applicable to the boundary. The Court in 1969
rejected the contentions of Denmark and the Netherlands on the
grounds that the Federal Republic of Germany had not ratified the
1958 Geneva Convention on the Continental Shelf, and was therefore
not bound by Article 6 of the United Nations Charter, thereby
putting the case outside Court jurisdiction.

CASE OF CERTAIN NORWEGIAN LOANS

France instituted proceedings in 1957 against Norway

concerning her obligations in respect to loans floated by Norway in France between the years 1885 and 1909. France maintained that the terms of the loans required payment in gold or certain other gold convertible currencies, rather than Norwegian kroner, because kroner was no longer convertible to gold. The Court ruled on July 6, 1957, that it lacked jurisdiction in the case because of the Norwegian right to invoke, by reason of reciprocity, certain French reservations in respect to its acceptance of the Court's jurisdiction under the optional clause.

NOTTEBOHM CASE

Liechtenstein on Decemer 17, 1951, instituted proceedings before the Court against Guatemala on behalf of Frederick Nottebohm who had been naturalized by Liechtenstein in October, 1939. Originally Mr. Nottebohm had been a German national but had been living, for the most part, in Guatemala since 1905. Nottebohm's claims concerned the application of war measures against his person and property by Guatemala in 1943. Guatemala contested Liechtenstein's suit, however, on the grounds that the 1939 naturalization process had not conferred the status of a neutral person on Nottebohm, because of the tenuous link between Nottebohm and Liechtenstein. Also, Guatemala denied that the Court currently had jurisdiction because Guatemala's original acceptance of the optional clause expired in January, 1952, before the Court could give a judgment in the case. The Court ruled in November, 1953, that it had jurisdiction because the Court had been seized with the matter prior to the expiration date of the optional clause. In April, 1955, it ruled against Liechtenstein, maintaining that the circumstances under which nationality had been granted were insufficient to enable Liechtenstein to present a claim in behalf of Nottebohm.

NUCLEAR TEST CASES

In May, 1973, Australia and New Zealand instituted proceedings against France and, in June, interim measures of protection were issued ordering France to avoid atmospheric nuclear tests in the territories of Australia and New Zealand. France has refused to accept Court jurisdiction. In July, 1973, the Court deferred its consideration of Fiji for permission to intervene in these proceedings. On December 20, 1974 the Court determined that the claims of Australia and New Zealand were no longer viable in view of the fact that France went ahead with the tests and, therefore, it was not necessary to render a decision.

RIGHT OF PASSAGE OVER INDIAN TERRITORY CASE

Portugal instituted proceedings before the Court on the grounds that in July, 1954, the Indian Government prevented Portugal's lawful right of passage to and between the Portuguese enclaves of Dadra and Nagar-Aveli located in Indian territory. The Portuguese claim was based upon: certain agreements concluded in the eighteenth century; actual practice over time in respect to the enclaves; and international custom in respect to such situations. A claim by India that the Court did not possess jurisdiction was rejected by the Court in November, 1957. In April, 1960, the Court decided that Portugal had the right of legal passage to and between the enclaves but that this right was circumscribed and did not include the right of passage in respect to arms, ammunition, armed police, and armed forces. The Indian behavior in terms of these limitations was found to be legal.

TREATMENT IN HUNGARY OF AIRCRAFT AND CREW OF UNITED STATES OF AMERICA

The United States instituted proceedings before the Court on March 3, 1954, against Hungary and the USSR concerning the treatment of a US aircraft and its crew forced to land in Hungary. Both the USSR and Hungary refused to give the Court jurisdiction in the matter and blamed the United States for the incident. The Court ruled, in July, 1954, that it lacked jurisdiction in view of the attitudes of Hungary and the USSR.

TRIAL OF PAKISTANI PRISONERS OF WAR (PAKISTAN vs. INDIA)

Pakistan instituted proceedings to obtain interim measures of protection for 195 prisoners of war and civilian internees held by India on charges of genocide. In May, 1973, the Court ruled that it must decide first whether it had jurisdiction in this instance; India, however, refused Court jurisdiction altogether. In July, 1973, Pakistan asked the Court to postpone action while the two nations attempted to reach a settlement. Said settlement having been reached, Pakistan requested the proceedings be dropped. In granting that request, the Court declared it need not debate the issues of jurisdiction as it was no longer being called upon to consider Pakistan's original request.

THE IRISH FISHING RIGHTS CASE

The United Kingdom instituted proceedings against the Irish Republic on January 3, 1974, concerning its extension of its fishing limits to 50 miles.

In July, 1974, the Court ruled that Ireland had broken international law in extending its fishing limits from 12 to 50 miles off the coast. Ireland refused to recognize the jurisdiction of the Court and ignored the judgment by extending its limits to 200 miles. (Norway also sought to extend limits to 50 miles because trawlers upset the sea catch.) (ENC. Britannica Yearbook 1975, p. 431)

THE AEGEAN SEA CASE

Greece instituted proceedings on August 10, 1976 against Turkey in order to obtan an immediate injunction preventing either nation from oil exploration in the contested continental shelf and from war preparations. The quarrel stemmed from the quest for Aegean oil which was discovered in 1973, and involved disputed airspace in the Aegean as well as Greek fortification of its islands near Turkey. Moreover, the dispute was complicated by the unsettled situation in Cyprus following the Turkish invasion of 1974. Turkey questioned the jurisdiction of the Court and boycotted public hearings on August 25-27, 1976, on the basis that Turkey had violated no law or agreement. On September 11, 1976 the Court ruled that the case did not require the use of Article 41 of the Statute, also that the matter of jurisdiction must be addressed. The Security Council urged direct negotiations between Greece and Turkey. After conferring with leaders from both sides, the President of the Court named April 18, 1977 as the date for submission of a memorial from both parties to the dispute. Greece claimed some islands to be within its national sovereignty that were within three miles of the Turkish mainland. Despite talks on oil and fishing rights at the Turkish embassy in Berne and talks on airspace rights at the Greek embassy in Paris, the dispute remains unsettled. While Aegean airspace remains in dispute, Greece began fortification of some Greek islands near Turkey and the latter sank a Greek boat on October 31, 1978. Turkey continues to consider the ICJ incompetent to rule on the issue of Aegean oil.

THE BEAGLE CHANNEL CASE

Argentina instituted proceedings against Chile concerning disputed islands in the Beagle Channel on July 7, 1977.

The Beagle Channel, an area located in southern South America between Argentina and Chile, was awarded to Chile. The decision was based on an interpretation of an 1881 treaty which gave Nueva, Picton and Lennox, all islands in the Channel, to Chile. Argentina has been unwilling to accept the decision, and, since both countries are predominately Roman Catholic, interceded to obtain the Pope's mediation, which Chile has accepted.

THE SCILLY ISLES AND CHANNEL ISLES CASE

In a second case during 1977, the ICJ considered a dispute between Britain and France concerning the continental shelf which they share, particularly with reference to the Scilly Isles and the Channel Isles. Each was awarded part of the territory; however there remained a long, narrow strip of sea area which had not been awarded to either side. Britain therefore returned to the Court for clarification of the disputed area.

THE ICAO CASE

India instituted proceedings against the International Commercial Airline Organization on August 10, 1975, concerning its decision to allow night flights from Pakistan to Bangladesh. India argued that its airspace treaty with Pakistan did not include night flights. The Court ruled that the treaty did allow night flights, but that the ICAO had no jurisdiction in determining airspace rights. The dispute was solved through bilateral negotiations.

THE IRANIAN HOSTAGE CASE

The United States instituted proceedings against Iran on December 3, 1979. The US argued that the capture and occupation of its embassy in Teheran, Iran was a violation of international law. Iran denied Court jurisdiction. The Court ruled that it did, indeed, have jurisdiction, that Iran had violated international law, and that the embassy personal should be released. Iran ignored the ruling.

THE SECRETARIAT

The Secretariat assists other organs; arranges for meetings; provides translation and documents; renders expert advice and assistance; and maintains the library services of the United Nations, constituting approximately 1,000,000 holdings at Geneva headquarters, and many more at the other 315 depository libraries. Members of the Secretariat are recruited from member states applying the highest standards of efficiency, competency, and integrity with due regard being paid to geographical distribution. In regard to this latter criterion and because of the General Assembly's policy guidelines which have pointed out previous maldistribution in respect to the Secretariat's staff, candidates are first considered from those states which have no nationals presently in the Secretariat. Secondly, they are recruited from those states in under-represented regions, designated as Africa and Eastern Europe; and, thirdly, they are recruited from those states in "over-represented regions," i.e., Western Europe. Once employed, staff members are expected to give their primary loyalty to the United Nations and may not seek or receive instructions from any government or authority external to the United Nations. Also, each member state of the United Nations promises to "respect the exclusively international character of the Secretary-General and the staff and not seek to influence them in the discharge of their responsibilities" (Article 100, Par. 2).

Presently---in order to maximize efficiency, continuity, and experience---fixed-term appointments, as compared to career appointments, are held to approximately 25% ot the total appointments.

As of December, 1979, the Secretariat consisted of 20,146 members, approximately 6600 of whom were serving in professional, manual, and field service categories. In addition, there were 4,000 technical assistance experts. Most of those in the Secretariat are regular members provided for in the budget; the remainder are members performing functions in connection with United Nations subsidiary organs, paid for by voluntary contributions.

The Secretary-General

According to Article 97 of the Charter, "the Secretariat shall comprise a Secretary-General and such staff that the organization may require." The Secretary-General is designated as the "Chief administrative officer of the organization," and in this capacity he exercises a variety of powers and engages in numerous functions. All of the staff of the Secretariat, for example, are appointed by the Secretary-General in accordance with the regulations established by the General Assembly. The Secretary-General sits in on meetings of the General Assembly, the Security Council, the Economic and Social Council, and other bodies and renders advice and performs functions which may be assigned to him. For example, he was given responsibility during the Suez crisis for composing the United Nations' Emergency Force and of directing it in conjunction with a group of advising states. The Secretary-General has also taken the initiative in efforts to mediate disputes, as in the Cuban missile crisis. His concern for political matters is clearly articulated in the Chapter where he is given the right to "bring to the attention of the Security Council any matter which in his opinion may threaten the maintenance of international peace and security" (Article 99).

The Secretary-General is appointed by the General Assembly (simple majority) upon the recommendations of the Security Council (veto applies). Because each permanent member of the Security Council possesses a veto over the recommendation, these members normally meet and agree on a candidate before full Council consideration. Under existing rules a deadlock between the Council and the Assembly is possible if the Assembly continually rejects the person recommended by the Council. Because the Charter is silent on the question of the length of term for the Secretary-General, the Assembly established a five-year term by resolution in 1946, with possible immediate reelection. After Trygve Lie's first term expired in February, 1951, the Assembly, on its own, extended his term for three additional years, in view of the Council's inablity to recommend a candidate to the Assembly. The Council was deadlocked on the matter. The USSR had vetoed Lie's renomination, because of his support of the United Nations' action in the Korean Crisis, and the United States had announced that it would veto any other candidate. The USSR viewed the Assembly's decision to extend Lie's term as illegal and refused to recognize him as Secretary-General. The supporters of the Assembly's action pointed out that the Assembly had originally set the five-year term and, thus, presumably, the Assembly could change it. Difficulties concerning the Secretary-General arose again during Dag Hammarskjold's active role in the Congo Crisis. This helps explain the "troika" proposal of the USSR to the effect that the Secretary-General's office should be replaced with a three-man directorate (each man with a veto) reflecting the three forces of the modern world--that is, the Western, the socialist (i.e., Communist), and the neutralist states. Basically, the USSR charged that Hammarskjold was favoring Western states in the Congo crisis. Various secretariat modifications were also suggested by certain neutralist states at the same time. The death of Hammarskjold, on September 17, 1969, and the election of U Thant, ended consideration of the troika proposal, which never received strong support, especially in view of Hammarskjold's opposition to it.

There have been four Secretaries-General: Trygve Lie

(1946-1952), Dag Hammarskjold (1953-1961), U Thant (1961-1971), and Kurt Waldheim, who began a five-year term of office on January 1, 1972. Waldheim was re-elected Secretary-General on December 8, 1976.

The permanent members of the Security Council have always received certain key positions in the Secretariat, in part, through gentlemen's agreements. Although the actual positions and their functions have changed over time, the concept of great power presence has persisted. Presently, persons from "great powers" hold, in fact, the following key positions: China, the Under-Secretary for Political Affairs, Trusteeship, and Decolonization; the USSR, the Under-Secretary for Political and Security Council Affairs; the United Kingdom, the Under-Secretary for Special Political Affairs; France, the Under-Secretary for International Economic and Social Affairs; and the United States, the Director of General Services and the Under-Secretary for Political and General Assembly Affairs.

Various officers and organs assist the Secretary-General in his work. These include, in addition to those already named: Executive Office of the Secretary-General, Office of the Assistant Secretary-General for Special Political Questions, Office for Inter-agency Affairs and Co-ordination, Office of Secretariat Services for Economic and Social Matters, Office of Legal Affairs, Department of Technical Co-operation for Development, Department of Administration and Management, Department of Conference Services, Office of Public Information, United Nations Center on Transnational Corporations, and Secretariat of the United Nations Conference on Science and Technology for Development.

THE CHARTER OF THE UNITED NATIONS

Note: The Charter of the United Nations was signed on June 26
1945, at the conclusion of the United Nations Conference on
International Organization held in San Francisco, and came into
force on October 24 1945. Amendments have been adopted for
Articles 23 (1965), 27 (1965), 61 (1973) and 109 (1968) and are
included in the text that follows.

The Charter of the United Nations

WE THE PEOPLES OF THE UNITED NATIONS DETERMINED

to save succeeding generations from the scourge of war, which
twice in our lifetime has brought untold sorrow to mankind, and to
reaffirm faith in fundamental human rights, in the dignity and
worth of the human person, in the equal rights of men and women
and of nations large and small, and to establish conditions under
which justice and respect for the obligations arising from
treaties and other sources of international law can be maintained,
and to promote social progress and better standards of life in
larger freedom.

AND FOR THESE ENDS

to practice tolerance and live together in peace with one another
as good neighbours, and to unite our strength to maintain
international peace and security, and to ensure, by the acceptance
of principles and the institution of methods, that armed force
shall not be used, save in the common interest, and to employ
international machinery for the promotion of the economic and
social advancement of all peoples,

HAVE RESOLVED TO COMBINE OUR EFFORTS TO ACCOMPLISH THESE
AIMS.

Accordingly, our respective Governments, through representatives
assembled in the city of San Francisco, who have exhibited their
full powers found to be in good and due form, have agreed to the

present Charter of the United Nations and do hereby establish an international organization to be known as the United Nations.

CHAPTER 1 --- PURPOSES AND PRINCIPLES

ARTICLE 1

The Purposes of the United Nations are:

1. To maintain international peace and security, and to that end: to take effective collective measures for the prevention and removal of threats to the peace, and for the suppression of acts of aggression or other breaches of the peace, and to bring about by peaceful means, and in conformity with the principles of justice and international law, adjustment or settlement of international disputes or situations which might lead to a breach of the peace;

2. To develop friendly relations among nations based on respect for the principle of equal rights and self-determination of peoples, and to take other appropriate measures to strengthen universal peace;

3. To achieve international co-operation in solving international problems of an economic, social, cultural, or humanitarian character, and in promoting freedoms for all without distinction as to race, sex, language, or religion; and

4. To be a centre for harmonizing the actions of nations in the attainment of these common ends.

ARTICLE 2

The Organization and its Members, in pursuit of the Purposes stated in Article 1, shall act in accordance with the following Principles.

1. The Organization is based on the principle of the sovereign equality of all its Members.

2. All Members, in order to ensure to all of them the rights and benefits resulting from membership, shall fulfill in good faith the obligations assumed by them in accordance with the present Charter.

3. All Members shall settle their international disputes by peaceful means in such a manner that international peace and security, and justice, are not endangered.

4. All Members shall refrain in their international relations from the threat or use of force against the teritorial integrity or political independence of any state, or in any other manner inconsistent with the Purposes of the United Nations.

5. All Members shall give the United Nations every assistance in any action it takes in accordance with the present Charter, and shall refrain from giving assistance to any state against which the United Nations is taking preventive or enforcement action.

6. The Organization shall ensure that states which are not Members of the United Nations act in accordance with these Principles so far as may be necessary for the maintenance of international peace and security.

7. Nothing contained in the present Charter shall authorize the United Nations to intervene in matters which are essentially within the domestic jurisdiction of any state or shall require the Members to submit such matters to settlement under the present Charter; but this principle shall not prejudice the application of enforcement measures under Chapter VII.

CHAPTER II --- MEMBERSHIP

ARTICLE 3

The original Members of the United Nations shall be the states which, having participated in the United Nations Conference on International Organization at San Francisco, or having previously signed the Declaration by United Nations of 1 January, 1942, sign the present Charter and ratify it in accordance with Article 110.

ARTICLE 4

1. Membership in the United Naions is open to all other peace-loving states which accept the obligations contained in the present Charter and, in the judgment of the Organization, are able and willing to carry out these obligations.

2. The admission of any such state to membership in the United Nations will be effected by a decision of the General Assembly upon the recommendation of the Security Council.

ARTICLE 5

A Member of the United Nations against which preventive or enforcement action has been taken by the Security Council may be suspended from the exercise of the rights and privileges of membership by the General Assembly upon the recommendation of the

Security Council. The exercise of these rights and privileges may be restored by the Security Council.

ARTICLE 6

A Member of the United Nations which has persistently violated the Principles contained in the present Charter may be expelled from the Organization by the General Assembly upon the recommendation of the Security Council.

CHAPTER III --- ORGANS

ARTICLE 7

1. There are established as the principle organs of the United Nations: a General Assembly, a Security Council, an Economic and Social Council, a Trusteeship Council, an International Court of Justice, and a Secretariat.
2. Such subsidiary organs as may be found necessary may be established in accordance with the present Charter.

ARTICLE 8

The United Nations shall place no restriction on the eligibility of men and women to participate in any capacity and under conditions of equality in its principal and subsidiary organs.

CHAPTER IV --- THE GENERAL ASSEMBLY

COMPOSITION

ARTICLE 9

1. The General Assembly shall consist of all Members of the United Nations.
2. Each Member shall have not more than five representatives in the General Assembly.

FUNCTIONS AND POWERS

ARTICLE 10

The General Assembly may discuss any questions or any matters within the scope of the present Charter or relating to the powers and functions of any organs provided for in the present Charter, and, except as provided in Article 12, may make recommendations to the Members of the United Nations or to the Security Council or to both on any such questions or matters.

ARTICLE 11

1. The General Assembly may consider the general principles of co-operation in the maintenance of international peace and security, including the principles governing disarmament and the regulation of armaments, and may make recommendations with regard to such principles to the Members or to the Security Council or to both.
2. The General Assembly may discuss any questions relating to the maintenance of international peace and security brought before it by any Member of the United Nations, or by the Security Council, or by a state which is not a Member of the United Nations in accordance with Article 35, paragraph 2, and, except as provided in Article 12, may make recommendations with regard to any such questions to the states concerned or to the Security Council or to both. Any such question on which action is necessary shall be referred to the Security Council by the General Assembly either before or after discussion.
3. The General Assembly may call the attention of the Security Council to situations which are likely to endanger international peace and security.
4. The powers of the General Assembly set forth in this Article shall not limit the general scope of Article 10.

ARTICLE 12

1. While the Security Council is exercising in respect of any dispute or situation the functions assigned to it in the present CHarter, the General Assembly shall not make any recommendation with regard to that dispute or situation unless the Security Council so requests.
2. The Secretary-General, with the consent of the Security

Council, shall notify the General Assembly at each session of any matters relative to the maintenance of international peace and security which are being dealt with by the Security Council and shall similarly notify the General Assembly, the Members of the United Nations if the General Assembly is not in session, immediately the Security Council ceases to deal with such matters.

ARTICLE 13

1. The General Assembly shall initiate studies and make recommendations for the purpose of:
   a. promoting international co-operation in the political field and encouraging the progressive development of international law and its codification;
   b. promoting international co-operation in the economic, social, cultural, educational, and health fields, and assisting in the realization of human rights and fundamental freedoms for all without distinction as to race, sex, language, or religion.
2. The further responsibilities, functions and powers of the General Assembly with respect to matters mentioned in paragraph 1(b) above are set forth in Chapters IX and X.

ARTICLE 14

Subject to the provisions of Article 12, the General Assembly may recommend measures for the peaceful adjustment of any situation, regardless of origin, which it deems likely to impair the general welfare or friendly relations among nations, including situations resulting from a violation of the provisions of the present Charter setting forth the Purposes and Principles of the United Nations.

ARTICLE 15

1. The General Assembly shall receive and consider annual and special reports from the Security Council; these reports shall include an account of the measures that the Security Council has decided upon or taken to maintain international peace and security.
2. The General Assembly shall receive and consider reports from the other organs of the United Nations.

ARTICLE 16

The General Assembly shall perform such functions with
respect to the international trusteeship system as are assigned to
it under Chapters XII and XIII, including the approval of the
trusteeship agreements for areas not designated as strategic.

ARTICLE 17

1. The General Assembly shall consider and approve the
budget of the Organization.
2. The expenses of the Organization shall be borne by the
Members as apportioned by the General Assembly.
3. The General Assembly shall consider and approve any
financial and budgetary arrangements with specialized agencies
referred to in Article 57 and shall examine the administrative
budgets of such specialized agencies with a view to making
recommendations to the agencies concerned.

VOTING

ARTICLE 18

1. Each member of the General Assembly shall have one vote.
2. Decisions of the General Assembly on important questions
shall be made by a two-thirds majority of the members present and
voting. These questions shall include: recommendations with
respect to the maintenance of international peace and security,
the election of the non-permanent members of the Security Council,
the election of the members of the Ecomomic and Social Council,
the election of members of the Trusteeship Council in accordance
with paragraph 1(c) of Article 86, the admission of new Members to
the United Nations, the suspension of the rights and privileges of
membership, the expulsion of Members, questions relating to the
operation of the trusteeship system, and budgetary questions.
3. Decisions on other questions, including the determination
of additional categories of questions to be decided by a
two-thirds majority, shall be made by a majority of the members
present and voting.

ARTICLE 19

A Member of the United Nations which is in arrears in the
payment of its financial contributions to the Organization shall

have no vote in the General Assembly if the amount of its arrears equals or exceeds the amount of the contributions due from it for preceeding two full years. The General Assembly may, nevertheless, permit such a Member to vote if it is satisfied that the failure to pay is due to conditions beyond the control of the Member.

PROCEDURE

ARTICLE 20

The General Assembly shall meet in regular annual sessions and in such special sessions as occasion may require. Special sessions shall be convoked by the Secretary-General at the request of the Security Council or of a majority of the Members of the United Nations.

ARTICLE 21

The General Assembly shall adopt its own rules of procedure. It shall elect its President for each session.

ARTICLE 22

The General Assembly may establish such subsidiary organs as it deems necessary for the performance of its functions.

CHAPTER V --- THE SECURITY COUNCIL

COMPOSITION

Article 23

1. The Security Council shall consist of fifteen Members of the United Nations. The Republic of China, France, the Union of the Soviet Socialist Republics, the United Kingdom of Great Britain and Northern Ireland, and the United States of America shall be permanent members of the Security Council. The General Assembly shall elect ten other Members of the United Nations to be

non-permanent members of the Security Council, due regard being specially paid, in the first instance to the contribution of Members of the United Nations to the maintenance of international peace and security and to the other purposes of the Organization, and also to equitable geographical distribution.

2. The non-permanent members of the Security Council shall be elected for a term of two years. In the first election of the non-permanent members after the increase of the membership of the Security Council from eleven to fifteen, two of the four additional members shall be chosen for a term of one year. A retiring member shall not be eligible for immediate re-election.

3. Each member of the Security Council shall have one representative.

FUNCTIONS AND POWERS

ARTICLE 24

1. In order to ensure prompt and effecive action by the United Nations, its Members confer on the Security Council primary responsibility for the maintenance of international peace and security, and agree that in carrying out its duties under this responsibility the Security Council acts on their behalf.

2. In discharging these duties the Security Council shall act in accordance with the Purposes and Principles of the United Nations. The specific powers granted to the Security Council for the discharge of these duties are laid down in Chapters VI, VII, VIII, and XII.

3. The Security Council shall submit annual and, when necessary, special reports to the General Assembly for its consideration.

ARTICLE 25

The Members of the United Nations agree to accept and carry out the decisions of the Security Council in accordance with the present Charter.

ARTICLE 26

In order to promote the establishment and maintenance of international peace and security with the least diversion for armaments of the world's human and economic resources, the

Security Council shall be responsible for formulating, with the assistance of the Military Staff Committee referred to in Article 47, plans to be submitted to the Members of the United Nations for the establishment of a system for the regulation of armaments.

VOTING

Article 27

    1. Each member of the Security Council shall have one vote.
    2. Decisions of the Security Council on procedural matters shall be made by an affirmative vote of nine members.
    3. Decisions of the Security Council on all other matters shall be made by an affirmative vote of nine members including the concurring votes of the permanent members; provided that, in decisions under Chapter VI, and under paragraph 3 of Article 52, a party to a dispute shall abstain from voting.

PROCEDURE

ARTICLE 28

    1. The Security Council shall be so organized as to be able to function continuously. Each member of the Security Council shall for this purpose be represented at all times at the seat of the Organization.
    2. The Security Council shall hold periodic meetings at which each of its members may, if it so desires, be represented by a member of the government or by some other specially designated representative.
    3. The Security Council may hold meetings at such places other than the seat of the Organization as in its judgment will best facilitate its work.

ARTICLE 29

    The Security Council may establish such subsidiary organs as it deems necessary for the performance of its functions.

ARTICLE 30

The Security Council shall adopt its own rules of procedure, including the method of selecting its President.

ARTICLE 31

Any Member of the United Nations which is not a member of the Security Council may participate, without vote, in the discussion of any question brought before the Security Council whenever the latter considers that the interests of that Member are specially affected.

ARTICLE 32

Any Member of the United Nations which is not a member of the Security Council or any state which is not a Member of the United Nations, if it is a party to a dispute under consideration by the Security Council, shall be invited to participate, without vote, in the discussion relating to the dispute. The Security Council shall lay down such conditions as it deems just for the participation of a state which is not a Member of the United Nations.

CHAPTER VI --- PACIFIC SETTLEMENT OF DISPUTES

ARTICLE 33

1. The parties to any dispute, the continuance of which is likely to endanger the maintenance of international peace and security, shall, first of all, seek a solution by negotiation, enquiry, mediation, conciliation, arbitration, judicial settlement, resort to regional agencies or arrangements, or other peaceful means of their own choice.
2. The Security Council shall, when it deems necessary, call upon the parties to settle their dispute by such means.

ARTICLE 34

The Security Council may investigate any dispute, or any situation which might lead to international friction or give rise to a dispute, in order to determine whether the continuance of the dispute or situation is likely to endanger the maintenance of international peace and security.

ARTICLE 35

1. Any Member of the United Nations may bring any dispute,
or any situation of the nature referred to in Article 34, to the
attention of the Security Council or of the General Assembly.
2. A state which is not a Member of the United Nations may
bring to the attention of the Security Council or of the General
Assembly any dispute to which it is a party if it accepts in
advance, for the purposes of the dispute, the obligations of
pacific settlement provided in the present Charter.
3. The proceedings of the General Assembly in respect of
matters brought to its attention under this Article will be
subject to the provisions of Articles 11 and 12.

ARTICLE 36

1. The Security Council may, at any stage of a dispute of
the nature referred to in Article 33 or of a situation of like
nature, recommend appropriate procedures or methods of adjustment.
2. The Security Council should take into consideration any
procedures for the settlement of the dispute which have already
been adopted by the parties.
3. In making recommendations under this Article the Security
Council should also take into consideration that legal disputes
should as a general rule be referred by the parties to the
International Court of Justice in accordance with the provisions
of the Statute of the Court.

ARTICLE 37

1. Should the parties to a dispute of the nature referred to
in Article 33 fail to settle it by the means indicated in that
Article, they shall refer it to the Security Council.
2. If the Security Council deems that the continuance of the
dispute is in fact likely to endanger the maintenance of
international peace and security, it shall decide whether to take
action under Article 36 or to recommend such terms of settlement
as it may consider appropriate.

ARTICLE 38

Without prejudice to the provisions of Articles 33 to 37, the Security Council may, if all the parties to any dispute so request, make recommendations to the parties with a view to a pacific settlement of the dispute.

CHAPTER VII --- ACTION WITH RESPECT TO THREATS TO THE PEACE, BREACHES OF THE PEACE, AND ACTS OF AGGRESSION

ARTICLE 39

The Security Council shall determine the existence of any threat to the peace, breach of the peace, or act of aggression and shall make recommendations, or decide what measures shall be taken in accordance with Articles 41 and 42, to maintain or restore international peace and security.

ARTICLE 40

In order to prevent an aggravation of the situation, the Security Council may, before making the recommendations or deciding upon the measures provided for in Article 39, call upon the parties concerned to comply with such provisional measures as it deems necessary or desirable. Such provisional measures shall be without prejudice to the rights, claims, or position of the parties concerned. The Security Council shall duly take account of failure to comply with such provisional measures.

ARTICLE 41

The Security Council may decide what measures not involving the use of armed force are to be employed to give effect to its decisions, and it may call upon the Members of the United Nations to apply such measures. These may include complete or partial interruption of economic relations and of rail, sea, air, postal, telegraphic, radio, and other means of communication and the severance of diplomatic relations.

ARTICLE 42

Should the Security Council consider that measures provided

for in Article 41 would be inadequate or have proved to be
inadequate, it may take such action by air, sea, or land forces as
may be necessary to maintain or restore international peace and
security. Such action may include demonstrations, blockade, and
other operations by air, sea, or land forces of Members of the
United Nations.

ARTICLE 43

1. All Members of the United Nations, in order to contribute
to the maintenance of international peace and security, undertake
to make available to the Security Council, on its call and in
accordance with a special arrangement or agreements, armed forces,
assistance, and facilities, including rights of passage, necessary
for the purpose of maintaining international peace and security.
2. Such agreement or agreements shall govern the numbers and
types of forces, their degree of readiness and general location,
and the nature of the facilities and assistance to be provided.
3. The agreement or agreements shall be negotiated as soon
as possible on the initiative of the Security Council. They shall
be concluded between the Security Council and Members or between
the Security Council and groups of Members and shall be subject to
ratification by the signatory states in accordance with their
respective constitutional processes.

ARTICLE 44

When the Security Council has decided to use force it shall,
before calling upon a Member not represented on it to provide
armed forces in fulfillment of the obligation assumed under
Article 43, invite that Member, if the Member so desires, to
participate in the decisions of the Security Council concerning
the employment of contingents of that Member's armed forces.

ARTICLE 45

In order to enable the United Nations to take urgent military
measures, Members shall hold immediately available national
airforce contingents for combined international enforcement
action. The strength and degree of readiness of these contingents
and plans for their combined action shall be determined, within
the limits laid down in the special agreement or agreements
referred to in Article 43, by the Security Council with the
assistance of the Military Staff Committee.

ARTICLE 46

Plans for the application of armed force shall be made by the Security Council with the assistance of the Military Staff Committee.

ARTICLE 47

1. There shall be established a Military Staff Committee to advise and assist the Security Council on all questions relating to the Security Council's military requirements for the maintenance of international peace and security, the employment and command of forces placed at its disposal, the regulation of armaments, and possible disarmament.
2. The Military Staff Committee shall consist of the Chiefs of Staff of the permanent members of the Security Council or their representatives. Any Member of the United Nations not permanently represented on the Committee shall be invited by the Committee to be associated with it when efficient discharge of the Committee's responsibilities requires the participation of that Member in its work.
3. The Military Staff Committee shall be responsible under the Security Council for the strategic direction of any armed forces placed at the disposal of the Security Council. Questions relating to the command of such forces shall be worked out subsequently.
4. The Military Staff Committee, with the authorization of the Security Council and after consultation with appropriate regional agencies, may establish regional sub-committees.

ARTICLE 48

1. The action required to carry out the decisions of the Security Council for the maintenance of international peace and security shall be taken by all the Members of the United Nations or by some of them, as the Security Council may determine.
2. Such decisions shall be carried out by the Members of the United Nations directly and through their action in the appropriate international agencies of which they are members.

ARTICLE 49

The Members of the United Nations shall join in affording mutual assistance in carrying out the measures decided upon by the Security Council.

ARTICLE 50

If preventive or enforcement measures against any state are taken by the Security Council, any other state, whether a Member of the United Nations or not, which finds itself confronted with special economic problems arising from the carrying out of those measures shall have the right to consult the Security Council with regard to a solution of those problems.

ARTICLE 51

Nothing in the present Charter shall impair the inherent right of individual or collective self-defense if an armed attack occurs against a Member of the United Nations, until the Security Council has taken measures necessary to maintain international peace and security. Measures taken by Members in the exercise of this right of self-defense shall be immediately reported to the Security Council and shall not in any way affect the authority and responsibility of the Security Council under the present Charter to take at any time such action as it deems necessary in order to maintain or restore international peace and security.

CHAPTER VIII --- REGIONAL ARRANGEMENTS

ARTICLE 52

1. Nothing in the present Charter precludes the existence of regional arrangements or agencies for dealing with such matters relating to the maintenance of international peace and security as are appropriate for regional action, provided that such arrangements or agencies and their activities are consistent with the Purposes and Principles of the United Nations.
2. The Members of the United Nations entering into such arrangements or constituting such agencies shall make every effort to achieve pacific settlement of local disputes through such regional arrangements or by such regional agencies before referring them to the Security Council.
3. The Security Council shall encourage the development of pacific settlement of local disputes through such regional

arrangements or by such regional agencies either on the initiative of the states concerned or by reference from the Security Council.
    4. This Article in no way impairs the application of Articles 34 and 35.

ARTICLE 53

    1. The Security Council shall, where appropriate, utilize such regional arrangements or agencies for enforcement action under its authority. But no enforcement action shall be taken under regional arrangements or by regional agencies without the authorization of the Security Council, with the exception of measures against any enemy state, as defined in paragraph 2 of this Article, provided for pursuant to Article 107 or in regional arrangements directed against renewal of agressive policy on the part of any such state, until such time as the Organization may, on request of the Governments concerned, be charged with the responsibility for preventing further aggression by such a state.
    2. The term enemy state as used in paragraph 1 of this Article applies to any state which during the Second World War has been an enemy of any signatory of the present Charter.

ARTICLE 54

    The Security Council shall at all times be kept fully informed of activities undertaken or in contemplation under regional arrangements or by regional agencies for the maintenance of international peace and security.

CHAPTER IX --- INTERNATIONAL ECONOMIC AND SOCIAL CO-OPERATION

ARTICLE 55

    With a view to the creation of conditions of stability and well-being which are necessary for peaceful and friendly relations among nations based on respect for the principle of equal rights and self-determination of peoples, the United Nations shall promote:
    a. higher standards of living, full employment, and conditions of economic and social progress and development;
    b. solutions of international economic, social, health, and related problems; and international cultural and educational co-operation; and

    c. universal respect for, and observance of, human rights and fundamental freedoms for all without distinction as to race, sex, language, or religion.

ARTICLE 56

    All Members pledge themselves to take joint and separate action in co-operation with the Organization for the achievement of the purposes set forth in Article 55.

ARTICLE 57

    1. The various specialized agencies, established by intergovernmental agreement and having wide international responsibilities, as defined in their basic instruments, in economic, social, cultural, educational, health, and related fields, shall be brought into relationship with the United Nations in accordance with the provisions of Article 63.
    2. Such agencies thus brought into relationship with the United Nations are hereinafter referred to as specialized agencies.

ARTICLE 58

    The Organization shall make recommendations for the coordination of the policies and activities of the specialized agencies.

ARTICLE 59

    The Organization shall, where appropriate, initiate negotiations among the states concerned for the creation of any new specialized agencies required for the accomplishment of the purposes set forth in Article 55.

ARTICLE 60

    Responsibility for the discharge of the functions of the Organization set forth in this Chapter shall be vested in the General Assembly and, under the authority of the General Assembly, in the Economic and Social Council, which shall have for this purpose the powers set forth in Chapter X.

CHAPTER X --- THE ECONOMIC AND SOCIAL COUNCIL

COMPOSITION

Article 61

1. The Economic and Social Council shall consist of fifty-four Members of the United Nations elected by the General Assembly.
2. Subject to the provisions of paragraph 3, eighteen members of the Economic and Social Council shall be elected each year for a term of three years. A retiring member shall be eligible for immediate re-election.
3. At the first election after the increase in the membership of the Economic and Social Council from twenty-seven to fifty-four members, in addition to the members elected in place of nine members whose term of office expires at the end of that year, twenty-seven additional members shall be elected. Of the twenty-seven additional members, the term of office of nine members so elected shall expire at the end of one year, and of nine members at the end of two years, in accordance with arrangements made by the General Assembly.
4. Each member of the Economic and Social Council shall have one representative.

FUNCTIONS AND POWERS

ARTICLE 62

1. The Economic and Social Council may make or initiate studies and reports with respect to international economic, social, cultural, educational, health, and related matters and may make recommendations with respect to any such matters to the General Assembly, to the Members of the United Nations, and to the specialized agencies concerned.
2. It may make recommendaions for the purpose of promoting respect for, and observance of, human rights and fundamental freedoms for all.
3. It may prepare draft conventions for submission to the General Assembly, with respect to matters falling within its competence.

4. It may call, in accordance with the rules prescribed by the United Nations, international conferences on matters falling within its competence.

ARTICLE 63

1. The Economic and Social Council may enter into agreements with any of the agencies referred to in Article 57, defining the terms on which the agency concerned shall be brought into relationship with the United Nations. Such agreements shall be subject to approval by the General Assembly.
2. It may co-ordinate the activities of the specialized agencies through consultation with and recommendations to such agencies and through recommendations to the General Assembly and to the Members of the United Nations.

ARTICLE 64

1. The Economic and Social Council may take appropriate steps to obtain regular reports from the specialized agencies. It may make arrangements with the Members of the United Nations and with the specialized agencies to obtain reports on the steps taken to give effect to its own recommendations and to recommendations on matters falling within its competence made by the General Assembly.
2. It may communicate its observations on these reports to the General Assembly.

ARTICLE 65

The Economic and Social Council may furnish information to the Security Council and shall assist the Security Council upon its request.

ARTICLE 66

1. The Economic and Social Council shall perform such functions as fall within its competence in connection with the carrying out of the recommendations of the General Assembly.
2. It may, with the approval of the General Assembly, perform services at the request of Members of the United Nations and at the request of specialized agencies.

3. It shall perform such other functions as are specified elsewhere in the present Charter or as may be assigned to it by the General Assembly.

VOTING

ARTICLE 67

1. Each member of the Economic and Social Council shall have one vote.
2. Decisions of the Economic and Social Council shall be made by a majority of the members present and voting.

PROCEDURE

ARTICLE 68

The Economic and Social Council shall set up commissions in economic and social fields and for the promotion of human rights, and such other commissions as may be required for the performance of its functions.

ARTICLE 69

The Economic and Social Council shall invite any Member of the United Nations to participate, without vote, in its deliberations on any matter of particular concern to that Member.

ARTICLE 70

The Economic and Social Council may make arrangements for representatives of the specialized agencies to participate, without vote, in its deliberations and in those of the commissions established by it, and for its representatives to participate in the deliberations of the specialized agencies.

ARTICLE 71

The Economic and Social Council may make suitable
arrangements for consultation with non-governmental organizations
which are concerned with matters within its competence. Such
arrangements may be made with international organizations and,
where appropriate, with national organizations after consultation
with the Member of the United Nations concerned.

ARTICLE 72

1. The Economic and Social Council shall adopt its own rules
of procedure, including the method of selecting its President.
2. The Economic and Social Council shall meet as required in
accordance with its rules, which shall include provision for the
convening of meetings on the request of a majority of its members.

CHAPTER XI --- DECLARATION REGARDING NON-SELF-GOVERNING TERITORIES

ARTICLE 73

Members of the United Nations which have or assume
responsibilities for the administration of territories whose
peoples have not yet attained a full measure of self-government
recognize the principle that the interests of the inhabitants of
these territories are paramount, and accept as a sacred trust the
obligation to promote to the utmost, within the system of
international peace and security established by the present
Charter, the well-being of the inhabitants of these territories,
and, to this end:
a. to ensure, with due respect for the culture of the
peoples concerned, their political, economic, social, and
educational advancement, their just treatment, and their
protection against abuses;
b. to develop self-government, to take due account of the
political aspirations of the peoples, and to assist them in the
progressive development of their free political institutions,
according to the particular circumstances of each territory and
its peoples and their varying stages of advancement;
c. to further international peace and security;
d. to promote constructive measures of development, to
encourage research, and to co-operate with one another and, when
and where appropriate, with specialized international bodies with
a view to the practical achievement of the social, economic, and
scientific purposes set forth in this Article; and
e. to transmit regularly to the Secretary-General for
information purposes, subject to such limitation as security and

constitutional considerations may require, statistical and other information of a technical nature relating to economic, social, and educational conditions in the territories for which they are respectively responsible other than those territories to which Chapters XII and XIII apply.

ARTICLE 74

Members of the United Nations also agree that their policy in respect of the territories to which this Chapter applies, no less than in respect of their metropolitan areas, must be based on the general principle of good-neighborliness, due account being taken of the interests and well-being of the rest of the world, in social, economic, and commercial matters.

CHAPTER XII --- INTERNATIONAL TRUSTEESHIP SYSTEM

ARTICLE 75

The United Nations shall establish under its authority an international trusteeship system for the administration and supervision of such territories as may be placed thereunder by subsequent individual agreements. These territories are hereinafter referred to as trust territories.

ARTICLE 76

The basic objective of the trusteeship system, in accordance with the Purposes of the United Nations laid down in Article 1 of the present Charter, shall be:
    a. to further international peace and security;
    b. to promote the political, economic, social, and educational advancement of the inhabitants of the trust territories, and their progressive development towards self-government or independence as may be appropriate to the particular circumstances of each territory and its peoples and the freely expressed wishes of the peoples concerned, and as may be provided by the terms of the each trusteeship agreement;
    c. to encourage respect for human rights and for fundamental freedoms for all without distinction as to race, sex, language, or religion, and to encourage recognition of the interdependence of the peoples of the world; and
    d. to ensure equal treatment in social, economic and

commercial matters for all Members of the United Nations and their nationals, and also equal treatment for the latter in the administration of justice, without prejudice to the attainment of the foregoing objectives and subject to the provisions of Article 80.

ARTICLE 77

1. The trusteeship system shall apply to such territories in the following categories as may be placed thereunder by means of trusteeship agreements:
   a. territories now held under mandate;
   b. territories which may be detached from enemy states as a result of the Second World War; and
   c. territories voluntarily placed under the system by states responsible for their administration.
2. It will be a matter for subsequent agreement as to which territories in the foregoing categories will be brought under the trusteeship system and upon what terms.

ARTICLE 78

The trusteeship system shall not apply to territories which have become Members of the United Nations, relationship among which shall be based on respect for the principle of sovereign equality.

ARTICLE 79

The terms of trusteeship for each territory to be placed under the trusteeship system, including any alteration or amendment, shall be agreed upon by the states directly concerned, including the mandatory power in the case of territories held under mandate by a Member of the United Nations, and shall be approved as provided for in Articles 83 and 85.

ARTICLE 80

1. Except as may be agreed upon in individual trusteeship agreements, made under Articles 77, 79, and 81, placing each territory under the trusteeship system, nothing in this Chapter shall be construed in or of itself to alter in any manner the

rights whatsoever of any states or any peoples or the terms of
existing international instruments to which Members of the United
Nations may respectively to be parties.

2. Paragraph 1 of this Article shall not be interpreted as
giving grounds for delay or postponement of the negotiation and
conclusion of agreements for placing mandated and other
territories under the trusteeship system as provided for in
Article 77.

ARTICLE 81

The trusteeship agreement shall in each case include the
terms under which the trust territory will be administered and
designate the authority which will exercise the administration of
the trust territory. Such authority, hereinafter called the
administering authority, may be one or more states or the
Organization itself.

ARTICLE 82

There may be designated, in any trusteeship agreement, a
strategic area or areas which may include part or all of the trust
territory to which the agreement applies, without prejudice to any
special agreement or agreements made under Article 43.

ARTICLE 83

1. All functions of the United Nations relating to strategic
areas, including the approval of the terms of the trusteeship
agreements and of their alteration or amendment, shall be
exercised by the Security Council.

2. The basic objectives set forth in Article 76 shall be
applicable to the people of each strategic area.

3. The Security Council shall, subject to the provisions of
the trusteeship agreements and without prejudice to security
considerations, avail itself of the assistance of the United
Nations under the trusteeship system relating to political,
economic, social, and educational matters in the strategic areas.

ARTICLE 84

It shall be the duty of the administering authority to ensure that the trust territory shall play its part in the maintenance of international peace and security. To this end the administering authority may make use of volunteer forces, facilities, and assistance from the trust territory in carrying out the obligations towards the Security Council undertaken in this regard by the administering authority, as well as for local defence and the maintenance of law and order within the trust territory.

ARTICLE 85

1. The functions of the United Nations with regard to trusteeship agreements for all areas not designated as strategic including the approval of the terms of the trusteeship agreements and of their alteration or amendment, shall be exercised by the General Assembly.
2. The Trusteeship Council, operating under the authority of the General Assembly, shall assist the General Assembly in carrying out these functions.

CHAPTER XIII --- THE TRUSTEESHIP COUNCIL

COMPOSITION

ARTICLE 86

1. The Trusteeship Council shall consist of the following Members of the United Nations:
   a. those Members administering trust territories;
   b. such of those Members mentioned by name in Article 23 as are not administering trust territories; and
   c. as many other Members elected for three-year terms by the General Assembly as may be necessary to ensure that the total number of members of the Trusteeship Council is equally divided between those Members of the United Nations which administer trust territories and those which do not.
2. Each member of the Trusteeship Council shall designate one especially qualified person to represent it therein.

FUNCTIONS AND POWERS

ARTICLE 87

The General Assembly and, under its authority, the
Trusteeship Council, in carrying out their functions, may:
    a. consider reports submitted by the administering
authority;
    b. accept petitions and examine them in consultation with
the administering authority;
    c. provide for periodic visits to the respective trust
territories at times agreed upon with the administering authority;
and
    d. take these and other actions in conformity with the terms
of the trusteeship agreements.

ARTICLE 88

The Trusteeship Council shall formulate a questionnaire on
the political, economic, social, and educational advancement of
the inhabitants of each trust territory, and the administering
authority for each trust territory within the competence of the
General Assembly shall make an annual report to the General
Assembly upon the basis of such questionnaire.

VOTING

ARTICLE 89

    1. Each member of the Trusteeship Council shall have one
vote.
    2. Decisions of the Trusteeship Council shall be made by a
majority of the members present and voting.

PROCEDURE

ARTICLE 90

    1. The Trusteeship Council shall adopt its own rules of
procedure including the method of selecting its President.
    2. The Trusteeship Council shall meet as required in
accordance with its rules, which shall include provision for the
convening of meetings on the request of a majority of its members.

ARTICLE 91

The Trusteeship Council shall, when appropriate, avail itself of the assistance of the Economic and Social Council and of the specialized agencies in regard to matters with which they are respectively concerned.

CHAPTER XIV

The International Court of Justice

Article 92

The International Court of Justice shall be the principal judicial organ of the United Nations. It shall function in accordance with the annexed Statute, which is based upon the Statute of the Permanent Court of International Justice and forms an integral part of the present Charter.

Article 93

1. All Members of the United Nations are ipso facto parties to the Statute of the International Court of Justice.
2. A state which is not a Member of the United Nations may become a party to the Statute of the International Court of Justice on conditions to be determined in each case by the General Assembly upon the recommendation of the Security Council.

Article 94

1. Each Member of the United Nations undertakes to comply with the decision of the Internatioal Court of Justice in any case to which it is a party.
2. If any party to a case fails to perform the obligations incumbent upon it under a judgment rendered by the Court the other party may have recourse to the Security Council, which may, if it deems necessary, make recommendations or decide upon measures to be taken to give effect to the judgment.

Article 95

Nothing in the present Charter shall prevent Members of the United Nations from entrusting the solution of their differences to other tribunals by virtue of agreements already in existence or which may be concluded in the future.

Article 96

   1.   The General Assembly or the Security Council may request the International Court of Justice to give an advisory opinion on any legal question.
   2.   Other organs of the United Nations and specialized agencies, which may at any time be so authorized by the General Assembly, may also request advisory opinions of the Court on legal questions arising within the scope of their activities.

CHAPTER XV --- THE SECRETARIAT

ARTICLE 97

   The Secretariat shall comprise a Secretary-General and such staff as the Organization may require. The Secretary-General shall be appointed by the General Assembly upon the recommendation of the Security Council. He shall be the chief administrative officer of the Organization.

ARTICLE 98

   The Secretary-General shall act in that capacity in all meetings of the General Assembly, of the Security Council, of the Economic and Social Council, and of the Trusteeship Council, and shall perform such other functions as are entrusted to him by these organs. The Secretary-General shall make an annual report to the General Assembly on the work of the Organization.

ARTICLE 99

   The Secretary-General may bring to the attention of the Security Council any matter which in his opinion may threaten the maintenance of international peace and security.

ARTICLE 100

1. In the performance of their duties the Secretary-General and the staff shall not seek or receive instructions from any government or from any other authority external to the Organization. They shall refrain from any action which might reflect on their position as international officials responsible only to the Organization.

2. Each Member of the United Nations undertakes to respect the exclusively international character of the responsibilities of the Secretary-General and the staff and not to seek to influence them in the discharge of their responsibilities.

ARTICLE 101

1. The staff shall be appointed by the Secretary-General under regulations established by the General Assembly.

2. Appropriate staffs shall be permanently assigned to the Economic and Social Council, the Trusteeship Council, and, as required, to other organs of the United Nations. These staffs shall form a part of the Secretariat.

3. The paramount consideration in the employment of the staff and in the determination of the conditions of service shall be the necessity of securing the highest standards of efficiency, competence, and integrity. Due regard shall be paid to the importance of recruiting the staff on as wide a geographical basis as possible.

CHAPTER XVI --- MISCELLANEOUS PROVISIONS

ARTICLE 102

1. Every treaty and every international agreement entered into by any Member of the United Nations after the present Charter comes into force shall as soon as possible be registered with the Secretariat and published by it.

2. No party to any such treaty or international agreement which has not been registered in accordance with the provisions of paragraph 1 of this Article may invoke that treaty or agreement before any organ of the United Nations.

ARTICLE 103

In the event of a conflict between the obligations of the Members of the United Nations under the present Charter and their obligations under any other international agreement, their obligations under the present Charter shall prevail.

ARTICLE 104

The Organization shall enjoy in the territory of each of its Members such legal capacity as may be necessary for the exercise of its functions and the fulfillment of its purposes.

ARTICLE 105

1. The Organization shall enjoy in the territory of each of its Members such privileges and immunities as are necessary for the fulfillment of its purposes.
2. Representatives of the Members of the United Nations and officials of the Organization shall similarly enjoy such privileges and immunities as are necessary for the independent exercise of their functions in connection with the Organization.
3. The General Assembly may make recommendations with a view to determining the details of the application of paragraphs 1 and 2 of this Article or may propose conventions to the Members of the United Nations for this purpose.

CHAPTER XVII --- TRANSITIONAL SECURITY ARRANGEMENTS

ARTICLE 106

Pending the coming into force of such special agreements referred to in Article 43 as in the opinion of the Security Council enable it to begin the exercise of its responsibilities under Article 42, the parties to the Four-Nation Declaration, signed at Moscow, 30 October 1943, and France, shall, in accordance with the provisions of paragraph 5 of that Declaration, consult with one another and as occasion requires with other Members of the United Nations with a view to such joint action on behalf of the Organization as may be necessary for the purpose of maintaining international peace and security.

ARTICLE 107

Nothing in the present Charter shall invalidate or preclude action, in relation to any state which during the Second World War has been an enemy of any signatory to the present Charter, taken or authorized as a result of that war by the Governments having responsibility for such action.

CHAPTER XVIII --- AMENDMENTS

ARTICLE 108

Amendments to the present Charter shall come into force for all Members of the United Nations when they have been adopted by a vote of two thirds of the members of the General Assembly and ratified in accordance with their respective constitutional processes by two thirds of the Members of the United Nations, including all the permanent members of the Security Council.

Article 109

1. A General Conference of the Members of the UN for the purpose of reviewing the present Charter may be held at a date and place to be fixed by a two-thirds vote of the members of the General Assembly and by a vote of any nine members of the Security Council. Each member of the United Nations shall have one vote in the conference.

2. Any alteration of the present Charter recommended by a two-thirds vote of the conference shall take effect when ratified in accordance with their respective constitutional processes by two thirds of the Members of the United Nations including all the permanent members of the Security Council.

3. If such a conference has not been held before the tenth annual session of the General Assembly following the coming into force of the present Charter, the proposal to call such a conference shall be placed on the agenda of that session of the General Assembly, and the conference shall be held if so decided by a majority vote of the members of the General Assembly and by a vote of any seven members of the Security Council.

CHAPTER XIX --- RATIFICATION AND SIGNATURE

ARTICLE 110

1. The present Charter shall be ratified by the signatory states in accordance with their respective constitutional processes.

2. The ratifications shall be deposited with the Government of the United States of America, which shall notify all the signatory states of each deposit as well as the Secretary-General of the Organization when he has been appointed.

3. The present Charter shall come into force upon the deposit of ratifications by the Republic of China, France, the Union of Soviet Socialist Republics, the United Kingdom of Great Britain and Northern Ireland, and the United States of America, and by a majority of other signatory states. A protocol of the ratifications deposited shall thereupon be drawn up by the Government of the United States of America which shall communicate copies thereof to all the signatory states.

4. The states signatory to the present Charter which ratify it after it has come into force will become original Members of the United Nations on the date of the deposit of their respective ratifications.

ARTICLE 111

The present Charter, of which the Chinese, French, Russian, English, and Spanish texts are equally authentic, shall remain deposited in the archives of the Government of the United States of America. Duly certified copies thereof shall be transmitted by that Government to the Governments of the other signatory states.

IN FAITH WHEREOF the representatives of the Governments of the United Nations have signed the present Charter.

Done at the city of San Francicso the twenty-sixth day of June, one thousand nine hundred and forty-five.